D0782976

EarthBound

Boss Fight Books
Los Angeles, CA
www.bossfightbooks.com

ISBN 13: 978-1-940535-00-5

First Printing: 2014

A brief portion of this book appeared on Kotaku.

Book Design by Ken Baumann

Page Design by Adam Robinson

EarthBound
by Ken Baumann

for Scott

FOREWORD

As ONE AGES, fond memories of times and places long since past become more and more precious. There are those memories I recall often: the first time I kissed my wife, my kids as small children when they were more fun than a bag of hammers, living in Tokyo at the height of the Japanese economic bubble ... And then there are those memories that return unbidden, triggered by a name, an image, a location. Lately, I've had many of those memories. Memories of a wonderful time in my life almost two decades ago, when I worked on *EarthBound*.

When I localized *EarthBound* for the North American market in 1995, I could already tell it was a special game. The story and gameplay conceived of by Shigesato Itoi was nothing short of brilliant, and I worked hard to do his vision justice. But it was released in a big box with a high price tag, and just didn't catch on with North Americans as it had in Japan.

For a while after the game's release, I didn't spend much time thinking about *EarthBound*. It was certainly a game that I was proud of, and I would occasionally be happily reminded of a character or moment in the game. But then I would also remember the reception it got when released. Sometimes it can take a few years to get over melancholy memories.

Then, more than a decade later, I slowly became aware of the *EarthBound* fan community. I occasionally looked at the forums and articles, and happily realized that *EarthBound* had a real impact on people's lives. For players, the game brought back memories of childhood, when the world seemed big, odd, and full of potential. Fans would replay the game, recounting stories of favorite moments, lines, and characters through online forums. I was fascinated by the feelings that the game brought out in fans. They said the game was charming and had heart, which was so often lacking in other games. And my memories of working on the game came flooding back as I considered the circumstances surrounding a line, a name, or a detail. It made me happy, and I felt good about my work on the game.

And so, after a few years of lurking on the fringe of the community, I decided to participate, and offered to help in any way I could, and the fan community's dedication to the game brought me into the fold. I have slowly begun to speak about my involvement with the game, and the response has been kind beyond my expectations. I've been embraced by the community, and their encouragement and support has made me consider many long-forgotten, happy moments. And more and more, I remember.

In the spring of 2013, Nintendo announced their intention to re-release *EarthBound* on the Virtual Console. I was shocked and thankful that the game would readily be available again, and especially happy that it would be enjoyed in Europe on a Nintendo system for the first time. When it was suddenly launched this summer, I was especially satisfied that the response I had hoped for in 1995 finally came true 18 years later. A new wave of *EarthBound* fans appeared, ready to try the game that their diehard friends had been talking up for years.

The fans' love for *EarthBound* never ceased to amaze me. I have seen amazing fan art, enthusiastic commentary about all portions of the game, and in-depth analysis of the localization work we did. I have watched *EarthBound* players live on streaming video, read player testimonies and personal histories on blogs, watched fans share secrets and insights over social media. And I have been told that, thankfully, the games text has aged well. For new and old fans alike, much of the pleasure to be found in *EarthBound* is to remember.

And now there is a new piece of fan appreciation for *EarthBound*—the book that you now hold in your hands. I am so thankful to Gabe and Ken for making this the first in the Boss Fight Books series. It is a humbling evidence of the place *EarthBound* occupies in players' memories.

Whether it is memories of people and places triggered by the game, times spent with other *EarthBound* fans, or just enjoyable moments from playing the game itself, those good memories are a vital part of the lure of *EarthBound*. I am humbled to have been a part of that. To borrow a well-known line from the game, I hope that all fans ultimately feel the same as I do: "It will always bring back the fondest of memories …"

Marcus Lindblom
Autumn, 2013

Arriving at each new city, the traveler finds again a past of his that he did not know he had: the foreignness of what you no longer are or no longer possess lies in wait for you in foreign, unpossessed places.

—Italo Calvino

199X

"I MEAN, YOU have to *pray* to beat an *emotion!*"

Scott laughs. "Yeah."

"How did this game get *made?*"

•

It's hard for me to reconcile *EarthBound* with any other video game I've played. Most popular games traffic in repetitive gristly thrills, but *EarthBound* focuses on emotion, on yearning. The team behind the *Call of Duty* franchise promotes the realism of its weaponry, implying their pride in its resultant gore, but *EarthBound*'s marketing campaign hinged on scratch and sniff stickers designed to evoke the smell of hotdogs and vomit. Hundred million dollar simulations of American hustle like *Grand Theft Auto V* are made by reclusive Lamborghini-driving auteurs and massive teams of developers, but I don't think there's a game that embraces and satirizes America's sentimental mongrel spirit better than *EarthBound*, which was produced by fewer than twenty people and helmed by an adman-turned-philosopher.

•

Not long ago, I called my older brother for the first time in a year. We spent time with each other when he was in town for my wedding, but except for a few text messages, we haven't spoken since June 2012. Major events have occurred in both our lives and I haven't called the guy. I felt and still feel bad about this. I thought this book about *EarthBound* would be the perfect excuse to get us talking again. Why I thought I needed a writing project to reconnect with my brother instead of any of the various quakes in our lives—familial death, lost jobs, new homes—is mysterious to me. Well, mysterious if I chalk it up to something more than "I'm just an asshole." So when I finally called him, I felt guilty.

But then I told him I was writing this book.

And then we started talking about *EarthBound*.

•

"I remember we got it, but we didn't play it for awhile," Scott says.

"Really?"

"But when we finally started we were obsessed with it. Played it all day on the weekends." I remember holing up in our bedroom with the shades drawn. The impressions the brown shag carpet formed on our thighs and feet.

"I'm curious … What do you remember the most about it?"

"The scratch and sniff cards in Nintendo Power—"

"Yes! Holy shit—" the smell of barbecue Lay's potato chip dust caked on the pads of my fingers. But what villain did that scratch and sniff scent belong to? I'm searching—

"And do you remember the Mr. Barf smell?"

"No—" *Carbon Dog!* Carbon Dog: That was the tangy offender.

"God, that was the *strangest* smell. I can't … I don't know how to describe it."

"Scott: For the sake of my book, you've gotta try." I laugh.

"Maybe like … a pickle. A pickle but grosser. You remember Twang Pickle Salt?"

"No." With one hand, I google Twang Pickle Salt. *ADD zing TO anything!*

"It smelled like that," Scott says.

•

I start up *EarthBound* and see three somber logos: Nintendo, Ape, Halken. Each white on black. The Ape Inc. logo is hard to make out, but it seems to consist of a scratchily drawn Neanderthal man holding a torch beside the word APE spelled out with bones. The next company, Halken, now known as HAL Laboratory Inc.—named after the brilliant and murderous HAL 9000 computer from the film *2001: A Space Odyssey*—reminds me of something, so I trawl the internet. I google *Terminator 2: Judgement Day*—a movie I watched about eighty-seven times as a child—trying to find the name and fictive logo of the company that manufactured Skynet, another cybernetic machine that tries to eradicate its master. The Cyberdyne Systems logo comes up but it's too pyramidal. I google "Warner Bros. 70s logo" and hit symbolic paydirt— the vintage WB logo is a prelude to Halken's dots and dashes, *and* it's designed by the legendary Saul Bass, a designer whom I've come to love while beginning my own work in book design. The tight synchronicity of this connection spooks me. But then it gets more intimate. As a fan of *2001: A Space Odyssey*, it's hard to look at the APE logo and not see a reference to the movie that blew my twelve-year-old mind more than any other filmic experience, a film that injected philosophical questions into my head that I didn't even know could exist.

EarthBound came out in the summer of 1995. I was five years old.

I don't know how old my brother was then, because I don't know how old he is now.

•

In 1992, when I was three, 1,441 souls lived in my hometown of Potosi, Texas. Over the next eight years, Potosi's population grew by 223 people.

I grew up on flat, windy, oil-rich land, and I grew up among animals. Lots of animals. We called it a ranch, and it was functional—my mother rehabilitated wounded animals, no matter the species, and bred and showed miniature horses. For about a year we raised Tater Tot, the world's smallest stallion. My mom snuck an acronym (that proved accurate) into his name: tot equaled "talk of the town." He was a popular little guy, often requested at various kindergartens or nursing homes in a fifty-mile radius. I've tried to recover some internet-bound record of Tater Tot's tiny prowess, but my search came up blank. But then I discovered another miniature horse named Tater Tot, who was documented by *National Geographic* as he visited hospitals and schools in Salmon, Idaho. Looking at that horse, I felt as if my past didn't empirically exist if it could not be salvaged with a Google search.

•

I can't remember much of my sixth year alive. I mean, I feel or can fill out impressionist activities, but all the memories lack climactic punctuation, erased and redrawn a million times by my attempts to see and sharpen the memory in the first place.

Allergies. High West Texan winds. Jumping on the trampoline. Raccoon paws and arrowheads. Watching huge flames eat up garbage in the concrete burn pit. Looking out the north window, full of fear.

Waiting for white, spindly clouds.

•

"It was a really mature game, though." Scott's enthusiastic now. "You had to be an adult, or maybe at least a teenager to get all the innuendos."

"Yeah, I remember it feeling naughty. I don't know if I even *knew* what naughty felt like then, but ..." When I was maybe eight, Scott called me upstairs to look at his computer, its monitor boldly in sight of anyone at the foot of the stairs, which was in turn near the front door to our house. I stood at the top of the steps and stared at the blinking MS-DOS cursor. *Pick a number,* Scott said. He grinned. *One through thirteen.* I paused, no idea what was coming. Thirteen, I said. Scott smiled, typed one then three, pecked Enter with his pointer finger, and revealed to me my first piece of pornography. And it would be privately mine (oh yes: *it would be mine*). I stared at the woman, a redhead wearing a leather holster that loosely arced across her hips, slung below her smooth white belly and sacral boobs and above her (very) bare bathing suit area. I now realize, as I glance at my redheaded wife across the room, that this memory is like an archaeological prophecy.

"And, it was an RPG, but it felt like a totally different genre." Scott says, snapping me out of it.

"Wait—what do you mean?"

"It was a lot simpler than most RPGs. There were only three core stats, only a few possible actions during battle sequences—the mechanics are really simple."

The mechanics.

I remember that Scott still programs video games.

•

The Super Nintendo looks like a pallid tank. The early video game consoles look undeniably utilitarian, as if the rush to get them to market provided time for nothing more than plastic housing and functional controllers. In fact, market pressures majorly shaped the Super Nintendo's precursor, the Nintendo Entertainment System, which was designed to look like VCRs in an attempt to distance itself from the catastrophic North American video game crash of 1983 (known in Japan as the "Atari shock"). In just two years video game revenues dropped nearly 97%. The structural evolution of gaming consoles, then, is not as linear as the march of Moore's law (i.e. the observation that computational power—via the increasing number of transistors on integrated circuits—doubles every two-to-three years); consoles have oscillated between geometric slot-full bricks and sleek sportscar-esque parabolas, molded by the projected desires of millions of young humans.

The Austrian architect Adolf Loos—a recipient of the philosopher Ludwig Wittgenstein's patronage—gave a lecture in 1910 titled *Ornament and Crime*. It's a wild text, narcissistic and riled and preachy, delivered by an architect-gone-ideologue in love with America. There's a line from the speech that went on to majorly impact architecture: *The evolution of culture is synonymous with the removal of ornament from utilitarian objects.* In the Villa Moller, a house Adolf designed in

1927, I see the blocky origins of the Super Nintendo. And later still, the ascetic empire of Steve Jobs.

Brilliant tools like smartphones are already pocketable basic shapes, so it's hard to imagine new forms for future video game consoles. Might they someday be terminally utilitarian, i.e. invisible? As ambient and protean as clouds?

•

"*Final Fantasy VI* had a bunch of different mechanics—it had the esper system, relics, custom moves for each character, real time input for certain moves in combat—"

"Oh, I see what you're saying. Yeah, you're right—there's something really elegant about *EarthBound*. It's like they decided to omit everything that would've distracted us from the characters and the story. And the really weird tone."

"Yeah: To play it well, all you had to do is grind, and all you had to do *to* grind is level up, restore your health, and upgrade your gear. Simple." I'm impressed by Scott's breadth of video game knowledge and by how comfortably he can deploy the lingo.

•

EarthBound's creator, Shigesato Itoi, first became famous for his slogans.

My favorite advertisement of his came out in June 1982, about a year before Nintendo released the Family Computer (colloquially referred to as the Famicom) in Japan. And unlike *EarthBound*, the ad is *stark*. It crystallized the Japanese public's intensifying antimilitarism, which stemmed from the Soviet war in Afghanistan and Japan's ominously incoming Prime Minister, one Yasuhiro Nakasone, director general of the Ministry of Defense. Published in the now-defunct magazine *Kokoku Hihyo* (literally "advertisement criticism"), Itoi's anti-war ad features a single white line of text and a photograph of two Japanese soldiers. Helmets shade their faces into half-anonymity. They bow slightly, their far hands gesturing beyond them to a gray backdrop. Their shadows are harsh and convex, like a hand painted Zen ensō split in half. Shigesato's slogan runs down the center of the image, stopping between the men's hearts. *"After you, Prime Minister."*

Shigesato's advertising career lasted decades, fueled by Japan's economic bubble of the 1970's and 80's. His other copywriting work is all over the place—advertising cars, jewelry, Suntori liquor, makeup, clothes, rock bands, and Studio Ghibli's animated films—and hell, even Woody Allen shows up. Shigesato's most iconic campaign, promoting the multi-floored Seibu department stores, consists of various photographs of Woody alongside the phrase "*Delicious life.*"

I can attest that Japanese department stores are as sensual and massive as Allen's neuroses. My wife and I travelled through Japan for our honeymoon, and during our stay in Tokyo we spent four hours in a branch of our favorite department store, Tokyu Hands. The store sports eight floors, and its wares rise in sophistication as you ascend its levels. It's a design fetishist's paradise and a total inverse of Dante's Hell. Second floor: suitcases and wallets. Eighth floor: stationary and "book reading supplies."

The malls in *EarthBound* aren't like the malls I grew up visiting. They don't sprawl out via long, store-crammed appendages, nor do they feature mall-looping designated power walker lanes. They rise.

•

"I think we started playing it on the weekends and we'd play it all day, every day."

I laugh. "Sounds about right. How long did it take us to beat it?"

Scott pauses. "Mmm ... Maybe two months. One to two months of eight to ten hours a day, or whenever mom walked in and was like, 'Go outside now.'" Is this where my predilection to binge-play video games and binge-watch television came from? Or is it merely formed by free time and technological ease (e.g. Netflix)?

"I remember playing it, but maybe I'm just making that up." I realize that, besides Scott's eyewitness testimony, I can never know if this is true or not. "I was five or six. Normally I'd just watch you play a lot of games, right? Like you were controlling a movie for us."

Scott's adamant. "No, we swapped back and forth."

Scott's seven years older than me. I remember this.

Twelve-year-old Scott passing five-year-old Ken the controller.

If you don't have an older brother, or if you have an older brother but he's not good to you, I'm sorry.

•

The logos disappear.

Eleven seconds into *EarthBound*'s opening, a high-pitched whine fades in. Red and yellow static fills the screen—a glitchy bloodstream. The whine is matched, doubled, synced—for fifteen seconds, it sounds like a chorus of car alarms, dying satellites, and falling bombs heralding chaos.

The static is replaced by an image of a city street at dusk. Cars and simple buildings line the road. A placard advertising the first resource most Americans clamor for in times of emergency—G A S—hangs on the building in the foreground, frame left. Three flying saucers mark the purple and yellow sky, each firing a ropey bolt of energy into the ground and distant buildings. The scene is letterboxed with odd concave lines, as if we're viewing it from within the safety of a visored helmet or some faraway theater. Capitalized red text at the top of frame reads: THE WAR AGAINST GIY-GAS!

At twenty-five seconds, the sky sparks. You *feel* these strikes, white light flashing in the painted sky and reflecting off the buildings, each scored with a thump of bass. The thumps come faster, tightening, non-rhythmic now. Explosions. The music is pure dystopia: minor notes and the disturbingly convincing sound of a panicked crowd—rioting or fleeing or both—and the lightning quickens, the explosions burst close together, the sky strobes and the sound rises—the whole screen going white—

Two seconds later, *EarthBound*'s jazzy and Latin-neighborhood-wakes-up-to-a-glorious-sunrise-after-a-nightlong-block-party-esque theme music sounds, the deco title card swings in, and you might be thinking: *What the fuck kind of game is* EarthBound?

EAGLELAND

IF *EARTHBOUND* IS the hospitable Milky Way, *Mother* is the experimental Big Bang.

In 1987, Nintendo took a pitch from Shigesato Itoi because of his copywriting work and, arguably, his fame. He brought his first written video game proposal to Shigeru Miyamoto—who had already created *Donkey Kong*, *Super Mario Bros.* and *The Legend of Zelda*—but Miyamoto's neutral reaction left Itoi in tears on the bullet train back to Tokyo. The next day, though, Miyamoto abruptly came around and development began on *Mother*, a peculiar game for Nintendo's Famicom.

Its title borrowed from the John Lennon song, *Mother* was released in Japan on July 27th, 1989, twelve days before I was born. The game sold about 400,000 copies and was a critical success, so development on a North American port (and a sequel) quickly began.

But work on the American version—now retitled *Earth Bound*—was beset by delays from an indecisive marketing department, and the port was eventually scrapped due to Nintendo's focus on the next generation Super Famicom console. Work on *Mother 2* for the Famicom was also scrapped, but eventually restarted for release on the Super Famicom, known as the Super Nintendo in North America. That game would go on to become *EarthBound*.

Nintendo's decision to push *Mother 2* to the Super Famicom was wise: The console attracted such a frenzy of consumers upon its release that the Japanese government asked Nintendo to schedule future console releases on the weekend in order to avert major dips in productivity, and the first shipments of Super Famicom systems to retailers were performed at night, warded from rumored Yakuza hijackers.

Mother is moodier than its sequel, and its gameplay is notoriously difficult, but how can you resist jumping in after this opening crawl (which feels right at home amid current mystery TV series):

> *In the early 1900's, a dark shadow covered a small country town in rural America. At that time, a young married couple vanished mysteriously from their home.*

The man's name was George, the woman's name was Maria. Two years later, as suddenly as he left, George returned. He never told anyone where he had been, or what he had done. But, he began an odd study, all by himself. As for Maria, his wife ... She never returned.

And then:

80 years have passed since then.

Mother's storyline and characters are obvious precursors to *EarthBound*'s, as is its adult tone—simultaneously sentimental and doomed, non-chronological and emotional—and its groundbreaking avoidance of the roleplaying games' sword & sorcery norms. At the time, few games were set in modern America (though I feel obligated to mention Square's obtusely racist RPG adaptation of *Tom Sawyer*, mercifully never ported to the United States). *Mother* is not an enjoyable game, really, but it founded the working relationships necessary for Shigesato to get *EarthBound* made. I respect the game for that, but from a distance.

Mother also marked the beginning of the collaboration between Itoi and his composer Keiichi Suzuki, frontman for the eccentric and innovative Japanese rock band, Moonriders. Oddly enough, I'd unknowingly listened to Keiichi Suzuki's other band, The Beatniks, but probably ten years after playing *EarthBound* by way of an Aphex Twin remix of the song "Une Femme N'est Pas Un Homme."

A woman is not a man.

Or, as Lennon puts it: *Mother, you had me, but I never had you.*

•

These little recurrent cultural wormholes—dubbed synchronicities by famed psychotherapist Carl Jung—could be considered potently meaningful (even if not causally related), or they could be viewed solely as examples of an unshakable confirmation bias. Regardless, each view evinces how tightly knotted experience is.

•

Nintendo's *EarthBound Player's Guide* is a 131-page document that originally shipped with copies of the North American game. I don't have the copy that Scott and I used (and abused via copious marginalia), but on the first page of my PDF copy of the *Player's Guide*, to the left of all the invisible Nintendo disclaimers—"Please read the following instructions thoroughly to

ensure the proper handling and use of your new game"
etc.—are six square screenshots from gameplay. The
third image down contains an early bit of in-game
dialogue that stands as the perfect introduction to the
EarthBound universe: "Could you sell me the mushroom growing on top of your head?"

•

And packaged in the back of the *Player's Guide*—
shamefully?—are the notorious *EarthBound*-themed
scratch-and-sniff cards. There are videos on YouTube
of cute kids scratching and smelling the 14-year-old
promotional cards, the scents—a busted imitation of
microwaved pizza, a gag-reflex-plucking mimesis of
hot vomit, the sweet whiff of some alien vegetable—
appearing to be as strong as ever.

Trying to forget those scent memories, I ask Scott,
"What do you remember the most vividly from the
game?"

And Scott says, "The song."

•

But before I dissect *EarthBound*'s wild array of musical styles and 16-bit vibrato, I have to let myself get
sidetracked by the Super Nintendo controller. I bought

an original so I could creepily caress it, this being the privilege of a writer doing research.

Its box features 3D-rendered animations of the cast of the *Super Mario Brothers* world, which is an odd box-art choice considering the 2D graphics of most SNES games. The only Super Nintendo game I played as a kid that attempted three-dimensions was *Star Fox*, which felt almost perfect in its technological spectacle. I revisit the game by looking at screenshots, and now my astonishment at the game is flattened. (I propose a corollary to Moore's Law, named after its most potent driver: Jobs's Law: The time between a product's agreed-upon novelty and its agreed-upon obsolescence halves roughly every two years.) *Star Fox* was alive with the spirit of technological sophistication, but now all I see are looping patterns from some janky Euclidean exercise.

Now, with twenty-three-year-old hands, the SNES controller's dimensions feels built specifically for me. It must've felt unwieldy when I was prepubescent. Now its buttons feel smooth and dead, as if they're pieces of corn-syrup-laden hard candies excavated a thousand years in the future. But the buttons pop and click when you press down, tacky and satisfying. The D-pad's got a texture that I puzzled at when I was younger—it feels pleasingly worn, as if some squishy automated hand gently used it to navigate through few hundred hours of games before it was packaged and shipped to its recipient, which in this case was a shelf (until I bought it on Amazon). If you've ever purchased a keyboard or a typewriter that reports back to you with its clicks, or enjoyed the warm vinyl pops elicited by a needle and a groove, then you've felt the tactile joy—feeling things touch other things to work for you—that an original SNES controller provides.

Maybe it's just the vague sense of spookiness I've felt since starting this book—no doubt seeded by trying to resummon the spiritual moments from my childhood—but this controller feels impossibly hollow.

•

When I tell Scott I bought an original SNES controller, he responds with:

Lol

Build one

And then he texts me a link to an online how-to full of schematics and diodes and cables.

Sometimes our unfamiliarity with each other is charming.

•

Until July 18th 2013, *EarthBound* was absent from Nintendo's eShop.

The story of *EarthBound*'s console revival is one of false starts, failed promises, and non-responses from Nintendo. But the re-release's long, difficult path has always been attended by *EarthBound*'s unceasingly enthusiastic and considerate fan communities.

Starmen.net is the fifteen-year-old hub of *EarthBound* fandom. It's a staggering networked monument to communal love. Innumerable angles of appreciation for the game are found within its digital walls. The Starmen.net community has lobbied Nintendo to rerelease *EarthBound* for *years*, waging letter-writing and call-in campaigns. The most impressive attempts to convince Nintendo to cater to *EarthBound*'s North American contingent, however, are their petitions.

Three times the Starmen.net community has, in their own words, "created, programmed, collected, checked, filtered, printed, bound, and shipped thousands of signatures right to Nintendo's doorsteps."

Their *Mother 3* petition, asking for Nintendo to release a North American port of the Game Boy Advance title, is a spiral-spined 819-page tome inscribed with 31,338 signatures, 1,200 of which are handwritten. And they bolstered this petition by packaging it alongside a handbound art album comprised of more than a hundred pages of fan-made *EarthBound* art, comics, and music. Starmen.net shipped these packages to Nintendo's Kyoto and Redmond offices, *Electronic Gaming Monthly*, and directly to Shigesato Itoi himself (at ludicrous international shipping expense).

Devotion, in the age of the internet, is best evinced by a collated, handleable object.

•

"That melody ..." Scott pauses, and in his silence I sense that he's hearing it again. Growing up, his pitch was so perfect as to cause him physical pain when he heard someone sing off-key, and now I'm thinking about all those times I sat shotgun while he drove, screaming along to "Lithium" by Nirvana or rapping along to tracks off *The Chronic 2001*. How my high-pitched inaccuracies, to which he didn't say a word, must've *hurt*.

"Yeah, I can remember most of it—" I say.

"And Giant Step. The cave with the blue guys, whatever they're called. The walking castle you walk around in."

"Oh, wow ... I'd completely forgotten about that."

"The trance in Saturn Village, when you have to go inside your subconscious ..."

"And what about the town that flips—becomes its reverse. Shit! I can't remember the name. Like it's this neon Twilight Zone version of itself—"

"Moonside."

"Yes!"

A beat. We collect ourselves, letting these new keys fit inside locks we didn't know still held in us.

Scott continues. "It all felt surreal. Totally surreal. Instead of just …" He goes quiet.

"Instead of what?"

"Instead of just *funky*."

•

When I tell people about my childhood, I'm continually surprised by their amusement. I forget that it's a little weird to have been raised in a house in which miniature horses sometimes slept (in diapers) on the couch in our living room. Or that to have inserted your forearms into an animal's vagina to retrieve its young is not a completely familiar—or conversationally comfortable—process to most people. Or that to sit shotgun while your father drove his homemade eighth-mile dragster nearly 200 miles per hour down a country road is exotic.

What felt strange to me then were actually the activities most entrenched in the environment outside my front door: religion and football.

If you've ever seen *Friday Night Lights* (the TV show), you've got a pretty hale picture of what Abilene, Texas and its satellite towns are all about. Growing up, it wasn't a question of if you were religious or not, but of which Christian denomination you belonged to. It wasn't a question of which sport you played, but of which position. Even then, sports other than football were simply that—Other. Not tagging yourself a Republican got you called a fag or a nigger-lover or hippie (and sometimes, worst of all, *a communist*). It's a land of grandmas who carry around "coonskin purses" made of actual human flesh flayed during the Civil War. (Yes, really.)

In a word, Abilene was often totally fucked.

That said, my parents—paternally atheist and maternally agnostic—were wonderful. I *did* find enclaves of empathy and cultural variety. And hell, most people I interacted with in Abilene were nice, just the kind of nice that might drive away in a truck painted with the Confederate flag.

•

I'm playing *EarthBound* in the same physical/spatial setup I had going as a kid, cross-legged and looking up at the TV. After tweaking the video and audio a bit, the game looks and sounds just right. Finding this precision feels devotional.

As the checkered background of the name-your-character screen appears, I start thinking that modern consumer culture Has It All Wrong. I mean, I'm playing *EarthBound* now on a big centerpiece TV, with the aural support of five surround sound units all pumping pristine digital sound. But when I was five, we played *EarthBound* on the small analog television in my bedroom, and it handled the sound adequately with two tinny speakers. I watched *2001: A Space Odyssey* on a TV not much bigger—scrambling back from the brand new DVD player to recline in a black leather chair (a piece of furniture that I begged for when I was thirteen, thinking it'd be "professional" to have a black leather office chair in the middle of my 10 x 9' bedroom, bisecting a room full of swords bought off late-night QVC commercials and thrift store collections of Choose Your Own Adventure books)—and the experience still felt totally immersive and tangibly life-altering. I doubt the immersion was crafted or aided by my blocky, ridiculously hard-to-move TV. But I was primed to fall into the artistic experience by my ritual (leather chair, lights off) and my intent (a curious, giddy anticipation for something new and mysterious). I didn't know anything about *2001* beyond what I imagined from its cover art. No looking up reviews in advance, no capping my expectations with critical comments from friends. No knowledge of the lead actor's personal life, the director's conversational oopses, the budget, or the marketing campaign. And it was the same with *EarthBound*. Immersion doesn't come with sophistication, or with gear. It comes with wide eyes and without any notion of limits.

It was with this psychological setup that I started this playthrough.

And then the door opened, the phone rang, my stomach churned, the dissatisfied cats, the hungrier dog, the sunlight, the thirst, *my health insurance*— adult life swirled in and around me like a sea that is impossible to calm.

That's a bit dramatic, but you get the idea. It's hard to maintain an unconditional openness to art when you've got a lot of shit to do.

•

"Was it a difficult game? I remember it being hard in spots." I don't yet remember specific examples of *EarthBound*'s difficulty, so I'm relying on a vague sense-memory of the sweat and stress-hormone cascades brought about by the game.

"There were a few spots, but no. Wasn't too bad."

"I mean, we didn't have the internet to consult, right? No walkthroughs."

"We had the guide."

"Right." I put my pen down for a second. "There's this book by Tom Bissell called *Extra Lives*. And there's this one part about him playing Metroid as a kid."

Scott makes a noise—yeah, talk about fucking difficult.

"And he's describing how he and his friend would just spend hours bombing the floor because there was nothing else to do. They were bombing the floor, over and over, and then suddenly a section of the floor opens up. And Tom starts crying with joy."

"Yeah," Scott says, laughing.

"I mean, *EarthBound* wasn't like that, right?"

"No, but man … Games used to be fucking *difficult*." There it is. "There were no tutorials at the beginning of the games—well, the instructions were the tutorial—and that was the norm. I remember this one game, this kangaroo game," which I eventually google and confirm that yep, it's indeed called *Kangaroo*, "on the 2600," the Atari 2600, released in 1977 in North America—and the first console I remember occupying space in my brother's bedroom—"and this game was *insane*. You were this kangaroo that had to jump and climb trees while all these monkeys throw apples at you, and each level gets exponentially more difficult, and it just progresses like that, getting harder and harder and harder."

"Like *Donkey Kong*?"

"But more of a pain in the ass." Scott pauses. "But that's what games were. That's what gaming should be. It *should* be hard. It should be a challenge, so that when you actually beat something it feels like a reward."

I recall my recent experiment with *Demon's Souls*, a stupidly difficult PlayStation 3 game that I played for an hour, put back in its case, and returned to Game-Stop the same day. To whichever federal agency that's tasked with designing new methods of torture: Your new scheme awaits at just $19.99 per copy.

•

I want you to play *EarthBound*.

Because I'm going to regale you with my playthrough, and that involves a lot of staring deeply into the game's plot and dialogue and emotional moments and quirks. If you'd like to experience *EarthBound* directly and unspoiled, go play it on a Wii U or shell out $200+ for the SNES cartridge. Or there are ROMs and emulators.

You can learn a great deal about yourself while doing something illegal.

•

My thirteenth birthday, Scott's upstairs bedroom, both of us snorting dainty stripes of crushed Ritalin and playing *Super Smash Brothers* in floating yogic trances until dawn.

•

The default choices in *EarthBound*'s name-your-characters phase bely the typical American kid's interests. There's a slight but fascinating cultural gap in *EarthBound*'s omission of pizza and its inclusion of salmon as a default "Favorite food." (In Japan's version of the game, the last pre-supplied choice for your favorite meal translates to "Dog Food.") The main character's first default name, his name in the *Player's Guide*, what Scott and I called him as kids, and the character's moniker in subsequent appearances in Super Smash Brothers, is Ness.

The last variable you choose is Ness's "Favorite Thing," and the category's last default choice is "Boxing." Scott and I might've started playing *EarthBound* the same day that Mike Tyson defeated Peter McNeeley—an underdog who stumbled up the ranking ladder into a lucrative bout with Tyson—in 89 seconds. That night we could've watched McNeeley's glazed eyes and wide pupils, knocked out on his feet.

We could've flinched at the force of the final punch.

•

You wake to the sound of a meteor whistling down to Onett long before sunrise.

Your room rumbles with its impact.

After a moment, distant sirens whine past your house and pause somewhere unseen.

You're in pajamas and topped with jagged black hair, appropriately mussed for your story's abrupt start.

You head downstairs. After a long and annoyingly knuckled staccato of knocks, Pokey Minch barges into your living room. Pokey's the rich kid next door, and he's an asshole and a kiss-ass. Soon enough, you realize his parents are cold and physically abusive. (I remember—with the precision of a lyrebird—the 16-bit bleat as Pokey's dad disciplines his children off-screen.)

The game's first party—you, Pokey, and your dog—set out to find Picky, the younger Minch brother.

•

I googled "minch" and the first result in Urban Dictionary—with 92 thumbs up and 69 thumbs down—is this: *Minch is the medical definition for 'stretched anal passage.'* The New Oxford American Dictionary, however, disagrees, defining it thusly: *A channel, divided into North Minch and Little Minch, separating northwest Scotland from the Outer Hebrides.* But the *Star Wars* wiki claims that: *Minch was a male member of a short-statured tridactyl species* (i.e. Yoda's species), *who served in the Jedi Order as a Knight of the Galactic Republic.* No conclusive clues here. Maybe Itoi wanted the obnoxious kid's name to play off the Yiddish word *mensch*, shorthand for a good person.

Regardless, Pokey's sprite design is … uncomfortably vulval. His eyes are concealed by a choppy blond bowl-cut, and his rump nose overhangs a vertical glyph of teeth.

•

In 1957, eight-year-old Shigesato Itoi accidentally watched a movie called *The Military Policeman and the Dismembered Beauty*. Produced by Shintoho Co. Ltd.—a Japanese movie studio that made more than 500 movies between 1949 and 1963, most of them low-budget and high-concept genre films—*The Military Policeman and the Dismembered Beauty* tells the story of the murder of a young maid named Yuriko Ito, and the subsequent hunt for her killer.

I've only seen the film in bits and pieces, but it contains some startlingly weird moments: At one point, Kosaka, the hero investigator, sits at his desk with Yuriko's lonely skull, monologuing to it like Hamlet. After a beat, Yuriko's face becomes superimposed on its former skeletal substructure and *stares* at Kosaka, prompting him to have an epiphany that leads Kosaka to Yuriko's murderer.

The film's also bookmarked by a scene that is—at first ambiguously—split in two. In its preface, Yuriko asks the titular military policeman, his face hidden, why he won't marry her, and then confesses to being pregnant with his child. After some tense silence in which Yuriko intuits his infidelity, she threatens to report his shameful behavior up the ladder to the squad captain, and the policeman quickly comes around and agrees to marry her. The film then cuts to the first half of the scene that Shigesato Itoi would later refer to as the "trauma" that inspired Giygas, *EarthBound*'s ultimate cosmic villain.

When the scene plays the first time, Yuriko and the policeman make love on a bank of grass, his face still hidden. But during the film's finale, the policeman— a thin Japanese Peter Lorre doppelgänger—confesses to murdering Yuriko, and his confession dissolves into the second half of the scene: The policeman pulls down Yuriko's top (exposing the white half-moon of her right breast), strangles her to death, dismembers her off-screen, and then has her straw-wrapped torso dumped in a well.

We can guess which half scarred the young Itoi.

•

Itoi's experience in the cinema mirrors Shigeru Miyamoto's experience in the cave.

From Nick Paumgarten's excellent profile on the creator of Princess Zelda and the Mario brothers:

> "[Miyamoto] explored a bamboo forest behind the town's ancient Shinto shrine and bushwhacked through the cedars and pines on a small mountain near the junior high school. One day, when he was seven or eight, he came across a hole in the ground. He peered inside and saw nothing but darkness. He came back the next day with a lantern and shimmied through the hole and found himself in a small cavern. He could see that passageways led to other chambers. Over the summer, he kept returning to the cave to marvel at the dance of the shadows on the walls."

Paumgarten later notes the irony that this natural and improvisational source of creativity would go on to lead subsequent generations to spend most of their playtime indoors while interacting with artificially structured and commodified entertainment. But it's also true that Miyamoto honored his experience in the cave by creating fantastic, interactive mythologies that have also inspired thousands—maybe *millions*—of people to express themselves in turn through art. Shigesato Itoi's experience in the cinema, then—similarly dark and magical by dint of cavernous space and projected light—was honored by *EarthBound*. And while both video game creators' experiences had to be severely simplified to become produceable, these products contain considerations totally absent in the impartiality of nature.

EarthBound is a story about a world invaded and manipulated by evil, but like boogeymen hiding underneath the bed, it's an evil that has been designed to be defeated by children. Unlike nature's impartial cataclysms and threatening storms but like the machinations of our imagination, at the end of the day, *EarthBound* can be powered off.

ONETT

IN YOUR FIRST battle of the game—whether you're fighting a Spiteful Crow or a Coil Snake—Pokey either complains to Ness, uses Ness as a shield, pretends to cry, smiles insincerely, plays dead, thinks to himself, apologizes profusely, tries to edge closer to the enemy, or "acts all innocent."

Despite Pokey's cowardice, you manage to weave your way through the overzealous and barrier-erecting Onett police force then to the top of a hill, where you find Picky slumped against a tree next to a half-buried meteor. The stone glows an orange rhythm.

Picky in tow, you cross the rock to return home, but a thin tract of gold light shoots out from the meteor and into the sky. The light widens, and a bee rises from within it.

The bee speaks. His name is Buzz Buzz and he's a messenger from the future, and he tells you that you have been chosen with three others to fulfill an ancient legend and defeat Giygas, "the universal cosmic destroyer."

You head home with your new insect companion but right before you cross the threshold of your white picket fence, a flash brings down your first substantial enemy, Starman Jr., a Gort-looking killer robot from the future with disconcerting snakelike arms and a hands-on-his-hips stance of machismo and disapproval. He is here to kill you and Buzz Buzz.

After a tidy battle—Buzz Buzz kicks his ass—you bring Pokey and Picky back home. Mrs. Minch sees the bee, freaks out, and—repeating that aural bleat you just heard as Mr. Minch punished his kids—swats your time-traveling telekinetic protector out of the sky. This moment feels emblematic of *EarthBound*'s entire tone: Grand storytelling gestures are quickly subverted by absurdity. It's a move that video games have wielded since the birth of the medium.

Buzz Buzz imparts some deathbed wisdom as he goes, urging you to find and collect eight melodies throughout the Earth that will allow you to channel your home planet's powers to defeat Giygas. Buzz

Buzz's last monologue ends, and his representative speck of pixels disappears with a wink.

And now you must set out as the prophesied baseball bat-wielding hero of a journey to save the world.

You are thirteen years old and you are alone.

•

Now that I've started the game, instead of writing about *EarthBound* I just want to play *EarthBound*.

While I play, I remain cross-legged on the floor, butt on a pillow, back against an ottoman, notebook and pen and bottle of water near my right knee. During my first few hours of play, I took three cramped pages of notes. So far, I've only written stuff addressing half of the first page. The game's like a monster that grows a new head each time I look away. My attention feels prohibitively narrow—can I capture my experience with *EarthBound*, both past and present, in its entirety? Should I even try?

In my notes, each line is a busted thought, a fragment. For instance: *Adults belittling Ness*—

Which is a recurrent thread in the game. From cops to dads, from strangers in fast food restaurants to local thugs, it seems that everyone's got an opinion about how out of place and helpless you are. (You're just a kid! What's a kid doing at a rock concert? What's a kid doing in Burglin Park? What's a kid doing talking to the *chief of police?!*) Making sure you feel belittled is a savvy narrative move—it's a necessary part of mythical structure. For most stories to effectively deliver their empathic payload, the hero's got to seem like the underdog. *EarthBound* reminds me of Pixar's movies, in that it's built to please kids and adults while strongly presenting the idea that kids—in their ability to trust each other, have faith, and be fearless—can be as heroic as their elders. Both *EarthBound* and Pixar films tell us that the underdogs can save the world by working together, and that they can return home with some vital part of their naivety untouched. And like most Pixar films—I'm thinking of the moment here where the toys in *Toy Story 3* join hands in the face of death—*EarthBound* allows itself to be deeply mature. Mature, but simple. The game's got a Zen master-goofiness to it. Like a dedicated monk, it's minimal with its mechanics (its action) and its graphics (its appearance). Some of the sillier Zen koans would be right at home among *EarthBound*'s dialogue. One of my favorites:

A monk asked Tōzan, "What is Buddha?" Tōzan replied, "Masagin!" [three pounds of flax]

As I slide further into this book, I slide further into the childlike desire to play.

•

This desire is redirected by trips out of town. My wife and I travel to New Orleans and New York, both trips marked by late nights spent bullshitting about literature and eating rich meals. I forget about *Earth-Bound* for a while.

A few days after we return home, though, I get a text message from GameStop reminding me about my preorder for *The Last of Us*, a blockbuster PlayStation 3 exclusive that Tom Bissell—my favorite video game critic—recently called a masterpiece. I pick up my copy but don't immediately start blitzing through it; I feel wary of playing a game other than *EarthBound* for the entirety of this project, afraid it might feel like cheating on my wife.

But I play it anyway.

Playing *The Last of Us* feels like inhabiting a world cruelly designed as *EarthBound*'s antithesis. *Earth-Bound* is wacky; *The Last of Us* is grim. *EarthBound* is relaxed; *The Last of Us* is stressful. *EarthBound* is cartoonish; *The Last of Us* is a monument to photorealistic apocalypse. As I sneak around a corner to stab a spore-mutilated humanoid with a homemade shiv for the hundredth time—I counted—my nostalgia for *EarthBound*'s goofiness flares up like the deep ache in your jaw when you're hungry for sugar.

•

The scientific evidence of what video games do to people is murky. The studies and meta-studies keep coming, piling on concern and calls for further research. Violent gaming has been linked to aggressive neural activity (and lessened activity in regions associated with emotional control), but playing certain specifically designed video games have *improved* cognitive abilities (like the ability to sustain attention) in elderly folks. In the conclusion to one study, its researchers butt up against a question that's been around since the dawn of human history: Do actual experiences and imagined experiences (such as dreams, hallucinations, and virtual simulations) affect us similarly?

It's been shown that American schizophrenics hear voices that are more violent than those haunting the heads of patients in Chennai, India. So how affected are neurotypical, non-gaming Americans by the ambient violence in American culture? Could we even calculate such saturation? And who would fit the criteria for an unsullied control group?

Once again, a nascent inquiry holds the slingshot, but it faces the looming, agile goliath of subjectivity.

•

When writing about a piece of art—be it a video game or a movie or a book—I feel a specific tension. It's part and parcel of creative anxiety—*this is no good, this doesn't need to exist, you're not equipped to write about this,* etc.—but it's a sensation that also feels uniquely warranted in our days of haste and ease of access. It's probably best summed up like this: Is what I'm writing just a lesser, narrower impression of the experience that the art can provide? Or, put more simply: Why am I dissecting this when someone can go experience and dissect it themselves?

As I stare at the notes from my second and third sessions of playing *EarthBound*—which is bringing back a familiar stiffness in my neck—I pause in fear. In doubt about the entire project. I know this kind of self-critical digression can be played up to comic effect—read a Geoff Dyer book or watch a Woody Allen movie—but the blur in my vision while staring at my little notebook feels indicative of a more destructive sadness.

As much as I fall into it and report back from *EarthBound*'s bubbly cosmos, I can never feel the exact wonder I felt when I was five. Nor can I summon with words the precise pleasure of playing the game itself.

According to John Gray in the introduction to his book *Straw Dogs: Thoughts on Humans and Other Animals,* progress—moral, philosophical, and political—is a harmful human myth. Gray writes:

"If the hope of progress is an illusion, how – it will be asked – are we to live? The question assumes that humans can live well only if they believe they have the power to remake the world. Yet most humans who have ever lived have not believed this – and a great many have had happy lives. The question assumes the aim of life is action; but this is a modern heresy. For Plato contemplation was the highest form of human activity. A similar view existed in ancient India. The aim of life was not to change the world. It was to see it rightly."

Or as Heraclitus put it: *Time is a game played beautifully by children.*

I've experienced *EarthBound* unbidden. Now I want to see *EarthBound* rightly.

•

Onett, Ness's hometown and the origin of your journey, is infested with punks. Members of Onett's local gang—The Sharks—roam around town and sprint into fights. The Sharks have a cohesive gangland aesthetic, albeit a weird one: The Yes Man Junior wears a purple full-body stocking accented with a skeleton design and wields a hula hoop as a weapon; the Skate

Punk sports a workmanlike combo of drab gray stripes, suspenders, and brown trousers while popping a frozen wheelie on a sharpened skateboard; the Pogo Punk ... well, attacks you with his pogo stick; and they all wear white gloves, huge grins, and a mohawk-esque spike on their heads. Appropriately enough to the me who grew up in Texas in the 90's—surrounded by country crooning and malicious mullets—the gang's ringleader and Ness's first solo boss fight, Frank, has a blond, greasy-looking mohawk/mullet combo.

You can't fight Frank, however, until you kick the butts of all local encounterable teens and bust your way through Shark HQ: the arcade. And if, as Ness, you express interest in joining The Sharks, you're told to "Come back after you finish *EarthBound*!", which isn't the *first* instance of *EarthBound*'s meta-awareness— that line being delivered by a cute blond girl outside Onett's library (which feels nice and Borgesian)—but it *is EarthBound*'s most infinitive instance of self-reference, as if it's a hint towards an open-ended amount of gameplay meant just for you. Even after you "beat" the game, you can still live within it ("Come play with us Danny. Forever ... and ever ... and *ever*.").

So now you're fighting Frank while a Johnny B. Goode knockoff anthem wails out in a chip-set tenor. If you're lucky you beat Frank the first time, but then you have to jump straight into a fight with Frank's tank-like robotic underling, Frankystein Mark II. (Which implies that a Frankystein Mark I exists in *EarthBound*'s unwritten prelapsarian prologue, and that maybe some altered version of you played through this prequel or is playing it *right now*, but only in your Platonic fantasies that are animated by all the artistic characters and events and environments you've encountered, the characters playing *with* and *amid* and *as* each other in a timeless, boundless ether; playing in the sweetest stakeless game.) And, funnily enough, Frankystein Mark II's got white gloves too, which makes Frank the only guy *without* gloves in the whole gang and the type of guy who *makes his robot wear gloves,* so it's good you just beat him, and it's good you beat his gloved robot, because you're a kid, and there's a world to save, and fuck those guys.

•

After taking care of Onett's entire criminal population with a baseball bat and a smidgen of psychic power, Onett's mayor gives you the key to the the "touring entertainers' shack." Touring performers being treated like shit is a recurring joke in the game, and encountering this for the first time as an adult who has worked as a professional entertainer makes me laugh. And so does Onett's mayor, B. H. Pirkle, after delivering a few lines that would be right at home in *The Wire*: "For someone as great as you, giving you the key could help keep the town peaceful. However, if you encounter a dangerous situation, please don't ask me to take any responsibility. I'll be able to avoid any responsibility, right?"

Corrupt Politician being a weedy and familiar trope cross-referenced by Tvtropes.org, a wiki that feeds and is fed by the culturally obsessive. Tracking the familiar moves and motifs of a piece of art, Tvtropes is an overwhelmingly analytical trove of info. And it has *EarthBound* marked as a participant in many common tropes and narratives, almost too many to digest in one sitting.

I dig Tvtropes's strategy for hiding spoilers—ruinous information is nestled by a dotted topless box and you must highlight it to reveal its white-on-white text; a secret presented as a ghostlike, irrevocable gift—but best of all are its names: Animate Inanimate Object, Ash Face, Big Damn Heroes, Spikes of Villainy, Nintendo Hard, Rodents of Unusual Size, and, my favorite, Quirky Towns, which features this explanatory note on the example section for *EarthBound*: "Let's see here … how about **all** of them?"

The protective nerd in me wants to say that Tvtropes is a symptom of humanity's desire to make encyclopedic the things it should keep sacred. If you play *EarthBound* fresh—without your critic hat on—and you win the lottery of aesthetic wonder, why risk irrevocably dissipating it with analysis?

Because my drive to see *EarthBound* as deeply as I can is greater than my comfort with simply enjoying it.

Simply put: Because I can't help myself.

•

I hope this project won't exorcise my ability to enjoy *EarthBound*, but I suspect it will.

•

After battling your way through Onett's caves, you reach a dark portal guarded by an unmoving Star of Bethlehem. It twinkles a murky light. You speak to it, engaging the Titanic Ant and his bug cohorts. The fight is simple but likely difficult. Regardless, you somehow proceed.

Your villain gone, you exit the cave to find your first sanctuary.

A huge footprint, marooned in grass.

The sky slowly pulses light.

You hear the first nine notes of your central melody.

Text appears: *Ness caught a glimpse of a small, cute puppy.*

•

The word *nostalgia* first appeared in a Swiss medical dissertation published in 1668, but the concept is ancient. While held captive on Calypso's island, Odysseus sits still on a rock and weeps, thinking of Ithaca. And, providing earlier evidence of archaic religion's yearning for return, Mircea Eliade argues that the central drive of *homo religiosus* is to reenact the creation of the universe; that all ancient religious rituals are stagings of the sacred moment of birth, or replays of mythical stories and adventures. So this yearning for a different quality of time—both dreamlike and sacred—is as old as Neanderthals.

This yearning isn't absent from the secular. As Eliade also shows in *The Sacred and The Profane*, the secular person still behaves in the grooves formed by religion. Which I'll personally cop to—our earliest myths were mimetic (you repaired your canoe because the gods repaired their canoe; you ate human flesh because the gods, unfortunately, ate human flesh)—because even though I don't consider myself religious, I find myself repeating the same stories over and over again. I'll watch a familiar movie to cheer myself up. I'll listen to the same song ten times in a row. I eat the same food because it's familiar, it's pleasurable. I keep routines, even if I don't call them sacred.

And I'm replaying an old video game. A video game that allows me—via my patient, unblinking avatar—to save the world.

To make the world anew.

•

You first hear her in a dream.

She tells you her name, says she's a friend. She asks if you can hear her.

My family first saw my little sister on a screen. Unable to have children the biological way, my parents fed their desire to nurture by looking at an adoption agency's website one Christmas break. They now claim that they weren't planning to adopt, but that the little girl in the first picture they saw—in the screen, on the website, in Siberia—was inevitably their daughter and my sister. That it was fated.

My mom and my grandma traveled to Moscow, gave stacks of money wrapped in paper bags to Russian bureaucrats and judges, then proceeded to the orphanage in Tobolsk. My mom was saddened by the children's daily diet of a weird green paste and by the cold they had been abandoned into, and she was sad because she couldn't adopt them all. They met Demi in person for the first time on Demi's first birthday. Demi—the name our family chose together months earlier—was a happy baby, and quickly fattened to a non-scary weight by real deal baby food and two doting parents. A few days after Mom and Demi arrived home, my mother told me and Scott that she had discovered more of Demi's history on the trip: Demi was born an identical twin, but the twin died at birth.

Demi, deriving from the Latin word *dimidius*, meaning *half*.

A fact we didn't know when we agreed that the name Demi just felt right.

December, 1996. Less than a year after Scott and I played *EarthBound* and rescued Paula together. Fighting our way into the next town to find the girl who spoke to us in our sleep.

•

Stuff like this means nothing or it means everything.

We're set amid these billion instances and we connect some if we're lucky.

TWOSON

The first sign you see reads: *Twoson—we got this name because we weren't first.*

•

Scott is seven years, six weeks, and a day older than me, and I'm seven years, six weeks and two days older than my sister. (I looked it up.) The biblical spacing between my siblings and I didn't portend to how we were raised, though. My dad is and was a staunch atheist, and my mother a happy agnostic. Around fourteen, Scott—my half-brother and the son of my mom's ex-husband—took up my dad's philosophical arms and accidentally combined them with a cocktail of teenage hormones and his brilliant, structure-hating mind, which lead to a short but hard period of drug use and backyard bomb-building.

Meanwhile, I was a clean-cut kiss-ass, charming every teacher and my parents by being a polite little egghead. And this baffled my parents; up until I was five years old, my mom and dad joked to friends that they were saving .money for college (for Scott) and bail (for me). Probably because I head-butted people when they tried to pick me up.

By the time we adopted Demi, I had become the necro-nerd who busies himself at his desk in third grade by drawing Spawn (the comic book antihero) and various situations regarding dismemberment, scattered human heads, troweled guts, explosions, dragons, wolves, etc. I had also taken to wearing mostly black to cop my brother's doomed fashion sense.

Scott and I watched a lot of anime—Cartoon Network in the late 90's played a daily afterschool block of golden era series like *Dragon Ball Z*, *Sailor Moon,* and *Gundam Wing* under the banner "Toonami"—and we played a lot of video games together before he moved up to high school and started spending time with kids who (quietly) claimed to be members of the Trench Coat Mafia.

•

As you guide Ness through Twoson, you'll pass a bunch of examples of the game's North American localization. These edits are either secular, puritanical, or legalistic—for instance, red crosses were removed from *EarthBound*'s hospitals after Nintendo discovered that the American Red Cross is litigious. Almost all references to religion, sex, murder, death, movies, and brand and band names are absent for English-speaking players. (All of these localization differences have been obsessively compiled by Clyde Mandelin—a staple of the online *EarthBound* community—at his site Legends of Localization.) One unintentionally awkward substitution: All references to booze were instead changed to coffee, a depressant-to-stimulant swap that often makes NPC behavior seem odd. Not all of the localization efforts were meant to dampen *EarthBound*, though; Legends of Localization features a table in which names of encounterable enemies in *Mother 2* and *EarthBound* put side-by-side, and the English names are much more evocative (e.g. the Care-free Guy becomes the New Age Retro Hippie).

As Mandelin says, "Game translations almost NEVER got this much careful treatment; just like Square's RPGs from the time, *EarthBound* was one of the earliest text-heavy console games to be given a truly serious, competent, and enjoyable localization."

•

"I mean, not many people quote lines from *Call of Duty*."

That's Marcus Lindblom, *EarthBound*'s main North American localization producer and translator. We're at the top of a conversation that'll last two hours.

Marcus' over-the-phone voice is hearty and authoritative. At certain points in our conversation, I feel like I'm talking to one of the gruff buzzcut guys who always seem to work at NASA in movies about the Apollo missions.

Marcus says, "*EarthBound* was very much a weird blend of humor and quirkiness, but also it's got this underlying tone of … you know, teaching lessons, almost. It's got a sort of deep, odd drama to it."

We riff on that for a bit, then I ask him the stumper: "Have you encountered anything since that feels similar to *EarthBound*? Something that pulls in stuff from so many disparate genres? It can be from any medium … movies, TV, books."

Marcus brings up *O Brother, Where Art Thou?*, the Coen brothers movie. I sense its similarities—the goofiness, the self-awareness, the moral lessons and mythological nods, the emphasis on music. But still, *EarthBound* feels *bigger*, maybe only because of the wider temporal boundaries that video games provide. Even a movie as large in scope as *Cloud Atlas* shows the seams of its material limits (I'm thinking of the prosthetic makeup and Tom Hank's inability to do a convincing, non-offensive accent). Though comparing *EarthBound* to even a three-hour long movie is unfair because *EarthBound* takes about twenty hours to play, not considering glitch-exploiting speed runs that take less than three hours. Role-playing games like *EarthBound*, then, are more temporally akin to long-running television shows, though neither are made without incredibly intricate (and strenuous) budgets.

"*EarthBound* was one of the hardest games I worked on," Marcus says. "We started around Christmas in '94, then worked heavily for three months on the writing. The English build wasn't even playable until March."

"So how'd the writing process work?"

"Well, the other translator I worked with, Masamuki Miyota, took a first pass at the text to just get it into broad-strokes English. And Japanese is a difficult language so it often would need a lot of work. Then I'd go over it and try to make sure the jokes worked, the puns, the references. And if they didn't, I tried to find something culturally similar enough to work for North American audiences. But it all happened really, really fast." Marcus laughs. "It's funny ... there's a text file out there on the internet, I think, of the *Earth-Bound* script, including some of its code. Well that's exactly what we had to work with. A lot of times, we couldn't see the line that came before the line that we were translating at the time, or we didn't have access to the original Japanese. We were sort of working in a black box."

This sort of baffles me, so I ask him about three times to confirm that this was truly the case. "So wait: did it seem like you were just translating non sequiturs a lot of the time?"

"Yes. But I hoped, at the time, that the weirdness of the game allowed me the latitude to get away with it."

Is the North American version of *EarthBound* truer to the tone Shigesato Itoi designed because of this black box translating? Marcus admits that the harried, opaque translation process made our version *weirder*— less profane because of the censorship, but more benignly eccentric.

This tone is exactly the element that stayed with me most as I grew up.

•

Twoson's the town from my childhood playthrough that I remember most cohesively, probably due to its hilariously domestic enemies—you fight the Ramblin' Evil Mushroom, Annoying Old Party Man, Unassuming Local Guy, Cranky Lady, and the aforementioned

New Age Retro Hippy. All of these battles are scored by a track appropriately titled *Battle Against a Weird Opponent* (which would make a great memoir title).

EarthBound's official soundtrack—only released in Japan—contains an hour of music split into twenty-four tracks. But *EarthBound* actually contains 170 tracks that take up a third of its 24-megabit cartridge. Though the complete in-game soundtrack takes up 183.5 megabytes on my computer, which is weird to consider, because 24 megabits—the largest storage capacity for Super Nintendo cartridges—is equivalent to just 3 megabytes. Or we can look at the game this way: Since 1 megabit = 1,000,000 bits, the entire world of *EarthBound* is manifested by 24,000,000 binary decisions.

To be able to casually interact with entertainment that complex and laborious still blows my mind, and deeper still when I remember that I was doing it as a kid, innocent of any given product's measure and human cost; I hadn't discovered the painful realities of capitalism first comprehensively described by Karl Marx, realities recently evoked by the collapse of a Bangladeshi garment factory (1,129 dead) and the Foxconn suicides (14 dead). And, like an iPhone or a t-shirt, piece of complex entertainment such as a video game or a feature film only exists when thousands of people labor for thousands of hours to make it exist. Rhythm & Hues Studios, a visual effects and animation company, filed for bankruptcy thirteen days before it won an Oscar for its work on *Life of Pi*. (A storied feature film producer told me that if his productions "don't bankrupt at least one VFX house, I haven't done my financial due diligence.")

And aren't children themselves a kind of complex entertainment?

•

"A mere milligram of the molecule could encode the complete text of every book in the Library of Congress and have plenty of room to spare," says an article by John Bohannon on Sciencemag.org.

So how many copies of *EarthBound* fit in a milligram of DNA? How many Ness's can dance on the head of a pin?

In January 2013, 739 kilobytes of information were encoded into a dust-like speck of DNA by the molecular biologist Nick Goldman and his team of researches.

A copy of *EarthBound* takes up 3072 kilobytes.

So at the standard that Goldman and his colleagues established, one gram of DNA could store 2,200,000 gigabits of information.

A single gigabit is equivalent to 125 megabytes. 125 megabytes means forty-two copies of *EarthBound*.

The human body contains about 250 grams of DNA.

So you or I could contain more than twenty-three billion copies of *EarthBound*.

Playing through every copy would take you fifty times longer than the age of the universe.

•

While exploring Twoson, you learn that Paula has been kidnapped. Everdred, the local crime boss, claims she was taken by a "chubby boy and a weird guy in a blue outfit" and that they're going to sacrifice Paula, their altar or idol unknown.

Alongside *EarthBound*'s explicit references to American culture, other game elements only seem obliquely referential (unless someday pinned down by Shigesato Itoi). For instance, I see Onett's white abusive cops and I can't help but think of Rodney King and the 1992 Los Angeles riots. Though Paula's disappearance from Twoson might be inspired by a horrible event that occurred much closer to home for *Mother 2*'s creators.

On November 13th 1990, nine year-old Fusako Sano disappeared from her hometown of Sanjō, 190 miles away from the offices where *Mother 2* was being developed. Her twenty-eight year-old captor, Nobuyu-ki Satō, forced her by knifepoint into the trunk of his car, drove her thirty-four miles to the house he shared with his mother, then imprisoned her in his upstairs bedroom for nine years and two months.

A disturbing opacity pervades events like this—lin-gering questions about Fusako's imprisonment, the in-nocence or participation of Nobuyuki's mother, or the ignored opportunities for escape—but the facts of the case seem more disturbing in their arbitrary, uncanny precision: how Nobuyuki attacked Fusako with a stun gun if she didn't videotape the horse races on TV, or how he carefully cut her hair, or how many of Fusako's meals were cooked by an unseen mother.

At the time, of course, Itoi couldn't have known Fusako's fate. All he or anyone else knew was that a girl was missing. But, for the secular, artists are considered respectable seers. So is this act of imaginative—or ac-cidental—prophecy surprising?

Another cursed jewel: a little more than a year after Scott and I completed *EarthBound*, and two days after Christmas, JonBenét Ramsey's autopsy revealed that she had eaten pineapple only a few hours before the murder.

These details.

I played *EarthBound* the first time without dwelling on the real-life tragedies that made the game's colorful kidnappings stick in my throat, without knowing that play only has gravity because of the danger it softly mimics. But now I'm able to plumb the decade that contained my childhood more impartially. I can see the latent unresolvable horrors that exist alongside me, waiting to be discovered by curious adults or people just doing their jobs.

•

More young American girls who were lost but became free again: Carlina White, Katie Beers, Jaycee Dugard, Elizabeth Smart, Gina DeJesus, Michelle Knight, Amanda Berry. Rescued by suspicion, accident, or self-inquiry.

You get to rescue Paula from a cult that worships the color blue.

•

1. Suppose I were to begin by saying that I had fallen in love with a color. Suppose I were to speak this as though it were a confession; suppose I shredded my napkin as we spoke. *It began slowly. An appreciation, an affinity. Then, one day, it became more serious. Then* (looking

into an empty teacup, its bottom stained with thin brown excrement coiled into the shape of a sea horse) *it became somehow* personal.

2. And so I fell in love with a color—in this case, the color blue—as if falling under a spell, a spell I fought to stay under and get out from under, in turns.

So begins *Bluets* by Maggie Nelson. The book, published in 2009, is gorgeous, discrete, and painful. I've read and reread and reread it. Documenting Maggie's obsession with (and obsession with documenting her obsession with) the color blue, the book lyrically moves from blue stuff to philosophy, from failed romance to carnal riddles, and, ultimately, into her paralyzed friend's new colorless pain.

The moment I guided Ness into Happy Happy Village, I thought of *Bluets*.

Exploring the town's cultish maladies as an adult brings to mind three real-world correspondences: the stalking Scientologist recruiters of Los Angeles, the friendly but pitchy solicitors outside Trader Joe's, and the bigoted paroxysms of Abilenean Christians. One of Happy Happy Village's NPCs asks you to donate to help her "protect the world from contaminants" and if you say no, she stalks you. You can converse with a blue-streaked cow who says that he'll respect Mr. Car-painter—the cult's leader—even if he's turned into a steak dinner. The local innkeeper tells you that "our policy is to only allow family members to stay here in the village. However, if you are interested in learning about Happy Happyism, we may make an exception," and if you refuse his services, he utters a line that seems right out of a Dostoevsky novel: "No faith ... No money ... You are a hopeless case."

Eventually, like the ATF unto the Branch Davidians—the siege of the armament-happy religious group's Waco headquarters occurring during *Earth-Bound*'s development—you wade into the devout belly of the beast. The Happy Happyism HQ is a large building filled with wall-to-wall indigo and hundreds of swaying, robed cultists. Their resemblance to garbed KKK members is obvious and apparently intentional; according to Marcus Lindblom, "They had *HH* on their head, which looked a little too close to a K because a lot of times, with really low-resolution fonts, a K and an H look really similar. There was no way I could let that one go. So I had them take the letters off and they put a little snowball on the end of the hat for me just to make sure it was as far away from the Ku Klux Klan as possible." Well, as far away from the Ku Klux Klan as possible they are *not*, but the change did steer the Klansmen garb away from representation and toward an uncomfortable homage.

If we were to take *EarthBound*'s early hours as material evidence of Shigesato Itoi's impressions of American culture, we would have to consider cruel parents, small-town gangs, abusive cops, weak-willed politicians, usurious property owners, and murderous religious cults as the case.

This does not seem inaccurate.

The cultists sway, and *Bluets* continues:

141. I have also imagined my life ending, or simply evaporating, by being subsumed into a tribe of blue people.

•

After defeating Mr. Carpainter, a yarmulke-topped llama of a man, the Happy Happyist spell is broken. The town and its residents return to their crisp green grass and corn-fed enthusiasms.

In short order, you've rescued Paula and gained a companion.

•

Not long after I freed Paula, Scott told me he got a new job in Denver and that he and Anna, his wife, were moving immediately. That night he texted me a photo of a sunset through a car window, testifying to how happy he was to ditch the confines of his old job.

And not long after that, I discovered St. John's College.

St. John's teaches the Great Books program. Created in response to the college's loss of accreditation, the Great Books core curriculum was first implemented in 1937. In four years, students blitz through the Western canon of mathematics, literature, theology, philosophy, and various sciences. You also study ancient Greek, French, and the rudiments of Western music. The school's professors are called "tutors" and forced to teach outside their fields of expertise. There are no regular lectures and no tests. Grades are kept but not used to judge academic progress. For four years, students read, write, discuss, and read some more.

While researching the college I realized a friend had gone to St. John's, so I emailed him a bunch of questions and anxieties. These sentences closed the first paragraph of his long response:

"Most of my life I've had the intuition that I was seeing things through peepholes. St. John's was the realization that the door could be opened, and that one could experience in full what one had only been spying on before. It was like being given permission to leave a shadowy world where one had to live on aspiration and voyeurism and entering a different one where scope was never constricted."

The next day, I scheduled a visit and booked a flight.

Santa Fe turned on all its charms while my wife and I were in town. Shooting stars, clear air, rhythmic thunderstorms—all its ecological beauty seemed to accent the ease I felt while sitting in on classes.

When I tell my friends about the campus tour, I equate the feeling of sitting in on classes with the feeling I had when I met my wife for the first time: *well, here is a perfectly inevitable opportunity made flesh.*

•

In the nascent days of this project, while researching the game, I realized that so much of the work ahead— presenting the history, mechanics and secrets of *Earth-Bound*—had already been done for me. The fan communities, be it Starmen.net or EarthBound Central or independent (and effusive) agents, have amassed a compendium that feels nearly comprehensive. There are certain blind spots in *EarthBound*'s developmental history, but they're blank due to the opaque nature of Japan's business culture. (If you want proof of this, try navigating a Japanese corporation's About section.) The temptation to insert secrets into unknown territories like these is hard to ignore and mostly benign, but it can also be catastrophic; just recall, from 2002, Donald Rumsfeld's epistemological justifications for invading Iraq:

> Q: "In regard to Iraq weapons of mass destruction and terrorists, is there any evidence to indicate that Iraq has attempted to or is willing to supply terrorists with weapons of mass destruction? Because there are reports that there is no evidence of a direct link between Baghdad and some of these terrorist organizations."
>
> Rumsfeld: "Reports that say that something hasn't happened are always interesting to me, because as we know, there are known knowns; there are things we know we know. We also know there are known unknowns; that is to say we know there are some things we do not know. But there are also unknown unknowns -- the ones we don't know we don't know. And if one looks throughout the history of our country and other free countries, it is the latter category that tend to be the difficult ones."

Is it simply a cop out, then, when I feel that the body of information available about *EarthBound*'s development is good enough to act on without my attempts to expand it?

And if so, is that okay in terms of this project?

What are mysteries—deadly or life-sustaining—if not prolonged attentions?

•

You work your way through another cave and defeat another overlarge animal to record the next four notes of *EarthBound*'s central melody. This time the magic is inscribed in a simple loop of tiny footprints, the Lilliput Steps—a nod to the race of tiny people in *Gulliver's Travels*.

You bring Paula back to her family and her fans. Ness is received as a hero once again.

After a brief interlude in which Everdred—the mustachioed criminal who warned you about Pokey's sacrificial plot—gives you a wad of cash totaling $10,000, you're free to head to Chaos Theatre to watch The Runaway Five perform.

The Runaway Five's obvious influence is The Blues Brothers. During localization, their black and white suits were made more colorful to avoid legal action from Universal Pictures or the film's producers. When I told my wife Aviva about this, she admitted she had never seen *The Blues Brothers* film. Having grown up on a steady diet of *Saturday Night Live*-spawned movies, I told her that her innocence here was blasphemous. That night, we marveled together at James Brown's hair.

•

When we give ourselves over to someone or something—a partner, a school, a cult, or a color—we do so out of the feeling that we've found a perfectly inevitable opportunity. For all our claims of agency, some circumstances feel so ripe as to feel impossible not to pluck and eat, a problem eloquently stated in the central text (and prop) of the most influential religion in the world.

Later on in *Straw Dogs*, John Gray states that "nearly everything that is most important in our lives is unchosen. The time and place we are born, our parents, the first language we speak – these are chance, not choice. It is the causal drift of things that shapes our most fateful relationships. The life of each of us is a chapter of accidents."

Elsewhere, he notes: "The cult of choice reflects the fact that we must improvise our lives. That we cannot do otherwise is a mark of our unfreedom. Choice has become a fetish; but the mark of a fetish is that it is unchosen."

In the case of *EarthBound* and other games, we are given a fixed set of circumstances and qualities to live with. While we can choose our hero's name and sometimes choose the shading of his or her final hours, we cannot radically alter the journey. Are games, then, the most accurate simulation of our unchosen lot in life?

THREE

I SAW IT in the video rental section of Albertsons.

I was five, maybe six. The VHS tapes were set on thin metal racks that lined an awkwardly oblong corridor in Abilene's nicest grocery store. Florescent tracks cast bright shifting glyphs onto the little tombstones of video entertainment. My mom would let me wander in and pick a movie to rent. And because I was raised with almost non-existent strictures on my media consumption, I always went for the box art that seemed violent, monstrous, or explosive. I now think that letting your child choose how to entertain himself—both in quality and quantity—is kind of insane. It's a parenting preference supported by the opinion that if you treat your child's agency with respect they won't misuse it, and I unequivocally misused it—and abused my parents' desire to spoil their kids—by becoming obsessed with collecting stuff, be it toys, or Pokémon cards, or *Spawn* comics, or *Choose Your Own Adventure* books, or swords and knives (it's hard to see the rationale of buying your son sixty pounds of swords and knives), or *Gundam Wing* models, or 1/60th model sports cars, none of which being sterling examples of human potential. I was enabled to rapaciously consume and to consume mostly junk.

It's hard to be sure which exact box art drew me in that day at Albertsons. Was it the edition with the cartoonish skeletal hand? Or the 50's style collage of the film's most perilous moments? Or the naked blue lady freaking out in front of the huge titular tombstone? Or the version with cheesy red letters, crappy stamp-like renderings of six male zombies, and what looks like Photoshop's default glow effect applied to almost every design element? Maybe I was snagged by this four-star praise from Leonard Maltin: "… the touchstone modern horror film. Don't watch this one alone!"

The film was *Night of the Living Dead*, and that is exactly what I did.

•

An obsession with zombie scenarios and zombie phenomena is very American and a little played out by now. So I won't bore you with my early zombie contingency plans, diagrams for escape routes, and coded locations of sharp blades, food, water, and gas. And the homicide pacts made with my parents and siblings and close friends. And my acute public awareness of rabies, twitching, fainting, pallid skin, blood-spotted collars and sleeves. And public sprinting, and lurching and— yeah. Yes. I won't talk about any of that stuff.

The zombie mythos infected me then, and for twenty years it has led me to some of the most gruesome entertainment I've ever enjoyed.

Which is why the town of Threed is so refreshing.

EarthBound's third major town has a ghoul and ghost problem, but some of Threed's zombies can speak to you, and often eloquently. Hell, even *charmingly*. The game evokes none of the monster-around-the-corner anxieties that are so well-exploited in contemporary games.

Later, when Threed's zombies are all trapped on a sort of zombie-retooled flypaper, I even empathized with the ruined human scourges, my belligerent obsession freshly ameliorated.

EarthBound tends to feel like a salve more often than an abrasive. Considered among the other media I gleaned before I lost the grace of a kid's self-unconsciousness, *EarthBound* stands out as feeling continually kind and reassuring. In this way, it is like a good parent.

•

Threed—called Threek in *Mother 2*, then translated away from another potential Klu Klux Klan association—is gloomy, dour and Halloween-themed. Its ghoul invasion stems from Master Belch, a massive anthropomorphic pile of vomit who you later must defeat. But before you can do that, your attention's caught by a barely-dressed blonde standing in front of Threed's hotel. She wears a black bikini—and sunglasses—at night. You follow this teased-hair tease into Threed's hotel, its muzak now lurching with an uneven tempo and jaundiced vibrato—following the woman who is so inhumanly thin that, while striding across the lobby, her legs are made of three diagonally-stacked flesh-toned pixels—and then she enigmatically disappears into the only vacant hotel room, and of course you follow her because this is a game and you *must* fall into its predestined traps to proceed, and the door closes behind you as zombies and zombie dogs and ghosts close in, and the screen begins to fade and you are struck by knockout stars and the same 16-bit bleat that Picky and Pokey Minch (and Buzz Buzz) were struck by, and then your screen … goes … black.

You wake up locked in an underground chamber, its floor a nearly perfect International Klein Blue. There's a door on the eastern wall so you try it but it's locked. Paula turns to face you, the player. The background fades to black as Ness and Paula ask for help, psychically calling for some guy named Jeff: Come save us, Jeff.

We need you.

We're your friends, but you didn't know it until now.

•

A musical interlude:

EarthBound's score could serve as a textbook example of how to smuggle eclectic, diverse musical styles into a piece of popular entertainment. Its biggest influence is the idiosyncratic and wide-band ethos of The Beatles' *Sgt. Pepper's Lonely Hearts Club Band*. Following that trail, *EarthBound* analysts have linked the score to other classics of late-60's and early-70's American rock, but also to music as disparate as Antonin Dvorak's *Symphony No. 9*, pre-Great Depression era ragtime, heavy metal, and Chuck Berry's poodle-skirt twirling rock and roll. As you progress through *EarthBound*'s successively odder levels and challenges, the soundtrack morphs—unafraid to jump genres—to fit and further the game's new elements, which seems like a bit of a miracle considering the crazily expensive orchestral scores in recent blockbuster feature films and AAA games. Today, most high-dollar scores only run alongside explosive set pieces or protracted battle sequences without really notating or accentuating the story, characters, or emotional scope. (And beyond the sonic wall of ur-blares in Christopher Nolan's latest films, I can't name a blockbuster score's motif in the last decade that has taken on a character of its own.)

Itoi, Kanazu, Suzuki and Tanaka worked hard to craft a score that is idiosyncratic, fun, emotional, and cohesive enough to accommodate the game's outlandish range of emotional intensity and cultural variety.

In the years between my first and current playthroughs, just a bit of a theme from *EarthBound* would conjure in me a flash of my childhood experience like some fractal strand of biographical code.

•

Years into work on *Mother 2*, Nintendo threatened to cancel the project. Development was taking longer than expected and the game was plagued with bugs and glitches. Originally, *Mother 2* was a project of Ape Inc. alone, but Halken—and Satoru Iwata, a talented

Halken programmer—came on board at the last minute to try to salvage the game.

In 2007, Itoi and Iwata—now Nintendo's long-standing CEO—sat down for a long conversation about work styles, *Mother 2*, and the challenges of game making:

Itoi: "To me, it seems that your methodology has been consistent as a programmer, and as president of Nintendo."

Iwata: "You think so?"

Itoi: "When the *Mother 2* project was about to fall apart, you came in to help, and this is what you said to us … 'It will take two years to fix this keeping what you have built up. If we start from scratch, it will take only a year. What do you say?'"

Iwata: "Yes, I remember." (Laugh)

Itoi: "We decided to start from scratch. You knew this was the best choice from the beginning though, didn't you?"

Iwata: "If I were to choose the best way at that time, yes, I would've started from scratch. But I wasn't in the project from the start, so I would've respected whatever decision you made. My task was to pull the project back together. Anyway, I think it was possible to do either way."

Itoi: "You thought it was best to start from scratch, and still you would've have gone either way?"

Iwata: "It was important not to ruin the atmosphere of the project team. You can't show up all of a sudden and destroy everything people have created until then. People aren't persuaded by such ways. The positive atmosphere of the team is crucial in order to succeed. I decided it was best to present the team with suggestions, and have them pick."

A bit later, Iwata concludes with this: "I like flying down with an umbrella to where people seem lost." And then Iwata and Itoi laugh together.

•

Ness and Paula's call for help drifts out of their underground cell, crosses an ocean, then winds through chilled pines and snowbanks to wake Jeff Andonuts, a thirteen-year-old boy with a blond bowl-cut and glasses that are perpetually frosted white. Jeff, spurred by this telepathic S.O.S., jumps out of bed, and his roommate Tony is quick to help Jeff escape their science-based boarding school. Tony fawns over Jeff, and it isn't meant to be subtle; in light of fan curiosity about the relationship, Shigesato Itoi confined: "I designed him to be a gay child. In a normal, real-life society, there are gay children, and I have many gay friends as well. So I thought it would be nice to add one in the game, too."

I'm sad that most video games are completely heteronormative.

Growing up runtish and secular in Abilene required hobbies. I began by collecting stuff, but my hoarding sensibilities faded and my desire to ham it up grew to take its place. I enjoyed school plays, and asked my mom and dad if I could do more theater. They supported the wish, and I ended up auditioning for a bunch of shows put on by Abilene's surprisingly vibrant community theater scene. Outside of school, I made my stage debut in *A Thousand Clowns*, a play about an unemployed TV writer who must care for his orphaned nephew.

But it was the next play that actually catalyzed the most substantiative change in me. Not as an actor, but as a person. The Abilene Repertory Theater was putting up a production of *A Midsummer Night's Dream*, and without ever having read Shakespeare before (and inspired by this idiot confidence), I auditioned. The theatre troop's honcho, a teddy-bear gent named Jeremy Henry, was impressed by the novelty of a fast-talking twelve year-old ringing his way through Elizabethan English, and he found a spot for me in the show. His angle: perform the play as if it were set in a Vaudevillian theater, its action set in the round. It was an ambitious design, but Abilene's stakes were so low as to transmute our all-inclusive anxieties of ambition into a childlike willingness to play (i.e. there were *a lot* of cast parties).

What I didn't know at the time is that participating in Jeremy's production would open up the world for me. Half the cast was either gay, lesbian, or bisexual. I had a crush on the girl who played Puck, and he has since undergone a female-to-male transition. I watched men kiss men and women kiss women, and, after a short period of perceptual rejiggering, I came to see these signs of affection as equal. Gaby became Gavyn, and friends were friends no matter their orientation.

There's something keen about the fact that Itoi inserted *EarthBound*'s only gay character in an England-esque land and not smack dab in Eagleland. The United States is only now catching up to Europe's wider acceptance for varied sexual orientations. I mean, I grew up in a town where "fag" and "nigger" were spoken casually. Bigotry can exist in explosive pockets anywhere on Earth, but rural life—lived without the metropolitan run-ins with people who do not share your fashions, orientations, and desires—tends to offer far fewer challenges to local norms, be they inspired, bigoted, or both in the same breath.

•

Jeff's journey through Winters is a perfect example of *EarthBound*'s peacefulness.

To journey south, you must charm a monkey with bubblegum, then wrap your way through tiny snow-dusted plateaus, fighting the occasional duck or ram until you near the edge of a lake. Its coast is kept by the Tessie Watching Society, a group of tent-bound voyeurs dedicated to sighting the legendary creature. After resting in one of their tents for the night, you walk back into the cold, but the score has shifted, and autumnal leaves blow in a gentle eddy. You walk to a patch of dirt dotting the end of a small finger of land, then your monkey companion asks for a piece of gum. After chewing it for a few seconds, he emits a large bubble and floats over the water like Mary Poppins, hovering over a promising whirlpool in the lake.

And then: Tessie emerges.

Purple and smiling—like Barney on a stiff dose of Valium—she glides toward you, volunteering to guide you across the icy waters. The music shifts again—now reminiscent of muted brass—as it marks this noble act of interspecies cooperation.

During this moment, I set my controller down and watched Jeff and the Bubble Monkey hitch a ride on Tessie.

I wasn't thinking about where to go or what to do next.

I simply listened to the melody, and the sound of the hypnotic tide.

•

A brief review of *EarthBound*'s dads:

Ness's dad is away on business and overworked, but he's always willing to talk to Ness on the phone and give him money. He's physically absent, but communicatively kind and concerned. If you play *EarthBound* for two hours straight, he calls to encourage you to take a break.

Picky and Pokey's dad is rich, usurious, jaded, and abusive.

Paula's dad is protective but clueless, unaware that Paula was missing days after she had been kidnapped.

Jeff's dad, whom you meet in his laboratory in Winters, is a full-blown mad scientist who dropped off Jeff at boarding school when he was three. When Jeff is reunited with him, Dr. Andonuts delivers the following monologue:

"Mr. Brickroad, the dungeon maker referred you, right? And not only that … What? Who? My son? Oh … I … can't … I can't believe it … You're Jeff, my son. It's been maybe 10 years since I last saw you. I'm so glad you're such a healthy boy. Uh, those glasses look good on you. How about a donut? Well, I was only offering … I'd also like a donut right about now. Have you already checked out Stonehenge? Well, at least I asked … Mmmm … mmhmm okay. By the way, why are you here? Oh, I see. That girl Paula must have sensed I was here. Ok, I'll try to help you out. I'm trying to make a Phase Distorter that can connect two points in space and time. It's still incomplete. I'll let you use another invention I call the Sky Runner. It's a little bit old but it'll certainly help. When you board, always listen for the message that comes from your destination. You'll get there for sure if you listen to the message. The round machine over there is the Sky Runner. What do you think? Isn't it neat? Get in! Let's get together again in 10 years or so."

So it's safe to assume that Shigesato Itoi wanted us to know that father–son relationships are fraught. But why is the distant father archetype so present in *Earth-Bound* (and in the entire Mother series)? Are distant dads more prevalent in Japanese family life than in American family life?

According to one recent study, Japanese fathers spend over an hour less time with their children on weekdays than American fathers, and they also spend significantly more time at work. Japanese fathers also believe that men belong in the workforce while women should look after the children more so than American fathers do.

These challenges, combined with the facts that Japan's fertility rate is one of the lowest in the world and that its median age is nearly the highest, have lead the Japanese government to spend more than thirty-billion dollars on family and childrearing support (and on campaigns like the Naga Prefecture's attempt to woo its single residents with pamphlets entitled "Marriage Story: Cinderella Story of the 21st Century"). To hit it right on the nose, *The Guardian* recently published an article headlined "Why have young people in Japan stopped having sex?".

So while the American image of the absentee father is accurate, it's a fierce competitor to the East.

•

When, in a conversation, Itoi's employee Yasuhiro Nagata suggested that the title *Mother* suggested "a parent watching over the children," Itoi agreed:

> "Yes, like a caregiver. Someone who doesn't say or do anything to interfere – just watches from afar. In one sense, I think that might be the ideal image of a parent.
>
> "I absolutely love the Pippi Longstocking stories. In them, her father is gone. He's a sailor who's gone missing. Despite that, Pippi is really strong and full of life. Her father's absence isn't used as a way to give the reader sadness to indulge in; instead, it's simply given as a fact of life as the story continues forward.
>
> "I think that might be the same thing here. That's why, looking back at the Mother series, I feel like I had a reason for making *Mother* 1 through 3. But now my kid is all grown up."

•

My mom and dad met in Mexico.

They were both vacationing there with their respective spouses. According to my mom's version of the story, she and Scott—then her husband and my brother Scott's biological dad—noticed *my* dad and his wife sitting in silence at a far table.

Half-jokingly (and whole-drunkenly (and probably much more than both those things but I totally don't want to unpack what my mom was thinking or wanting at that time)), my mom said to Scott, "She looks like your type, right?"

Scott responded: "And he looks like yours."

Eventually, the tables—and couples—swapped.

Messily, of course. According to both my mom and my dad, it took my dad threatening to drive to Lake Tahoe to kidnap my mom and little Scott at gunpoint to finally swap the couples for good.

A few years later, I was born of this new configuration.

Miraculously, both couples—Vicki and Bob; Gretchen and Scott—have stayed together since.

It's a wild story that's become my stock tall tale to use at parties, and it's nice that I don't have to embellish any details (e.g. cocaine, Mexico, guns).

But the atypical nature of my parent's relationship—and its resemblance to the relationship between Ness's parents—doesn't stop there.

•

When I was ten, I found an ad for a small-town "actor/model search" in the classifieds. The next day, while swatting away nickel-sized mosquitoes and competitively annoying wasps in our backyard, I asked mom if I could go. After examining the ad and talking to my dad, they agreed to take me.

I don't remember much from this small-town convention beyond the con itself: charging my parents a few hundred dollars for me to "progress to the next level." Mom and dad ponied up, and the next level consisted of a daylong kiddie meat-market held in a massive, florescent-lit hotel ballroom bisected by a long, platformed, and carpeted runway. Each kid was instructed to walk—"naturally"—down the runway and then go talk to any of the agents who called them over from behind their shared eighth-mile-long table.

I walked and then I talked.

The agent who wanted to speak to me worked for a talent agency in New York City. She, fishing to see if I had the commodifiable ability to enthuse, asked what I was currently interested in. This was an excuse for me to talk about Pokémon, *and talk about Pokémon I did*. Ten to ten-thousand minutes later, she offered to represent me. I remember the thrill of that moment, of knowing that I had just convinced an adult to invite me to adventure out to the city that I had been obsessed with for years. (My best friend's older brother feigned at being an Italian mobster, which made me want to be an Italian mobster, which lead to an obsession with Sinatra and *Goodfellas* and reading about the Sicilian mafia's spectacular rise and fall in NYC, all of which sort of crystallizing into a general and persistent desire to live in the city.)

Six months later, my mom moved me and my little sister to the Lower East Side for two months. She carted me and Demi to my first commercial auditions, patiently waiting in the cramped lobbies and hallways while I hammed it up in front of klieg lights, camcorders, and casting directors. I also auditioned for my first print modeling jobs, which involved having my picture taken a few times and writing down my clothing sizes on an index card. And I got my first headshots, freezing my little ass off on an NYC rooftop in February while wearing makeup (typical), angel wings (don't ask), and an outfit appropriate for a middle-aged college administrator (I have no idea). In our rented three-hundred square feet studio apartment, I'd read and do homework from my school in Abilene, and my mom would trawl eBay with her primitive laptop and dial-up connection. The whole trip was subsidized by the money my dad made by fixing cars back home.

Two months later, we returned to the ranch. I hadn't found work.

But then my agent in New York set me up to meet an agent in Dallas. Eventually, I started auditioning for non-commercials and print modeling work for companies like JCPenney and Dilliard's, and then I started booking work. I fervently articulated action figures in carefully orchestrated close-ups for Hasbro; I smiled until my face hurt to advertise jeans and t-shirts; I beat my father's head in with a baseball bat to emotionally punctuate a student film. It all felt incredible and exotic, this working (and getting paid) thing. At my parents' behest I saved most of my money but used the discretionary cash to buy action movies, Offspring CDs, and Pokémon and Magic: The Gathering cards, thus completing the positive feedback loop of work, get paid, then purchase. This whole Dallas-bound enterprise required my mom to drive me three and a half hours (each way) from Abilene to Dallas and then back, as well as convincing my teachers to let me miss four days of school per week as long as I did all of my homework and didn't miss any tests.

After about three years of this, my agent recommended we go to Los Angeles for pilot season, during which all of the major TV networks produced their slates of pilot episodes for potential new series.

This, as my family and I knew, would be the big gamble.

•

Around the time of *EarthBound* and *Night of the Living Dead*, I also watched each of the *Ernest* movies. So last night, in the name of further dissecting my childhood obsessions, I watched *Ernest Scared Stupid* for the first and probably only time as an adult.

Before clicking play, I wrote down my memories of the film, feeling that they would be mostly accurate. The vividness of my memories of the movie seemed indistinguishable from its truth, a familiar problem to lawyers questioning an eyewitness. There are many images I thought I remembered from *Ernest Scared Stupid*, but the most alive impressions were of boogers and goofy faces.

I feel that I should summarize *Ernest Scared Stupid*'s plot for the layman (although I'm tempted to cut and paste the entire plot summary from Wikipedia, which happens to be one of the most straight-faced texts I've ever read, and accidentally on par with Andy Kaufman's work): Ernest, a lovable garbageman with multiple personality disorder, decides to help a trio of bullied children by building them a tree house. In the process, he disturbs an ancient demon previously buried underneath the chosen (spooky) tree by Ernest's ancestor. The demon appears, troll-like, covered in snot, and dedicated to turning five children into wooden dolls, the complete set of which forming a sort of key that unlocks the existential capacities of his troll children. After close to an hour of bumbling around and lousing up stuff, Ernest decides to fight the trolls, crying out, "Someone with a runny nose is gonna die!" At first, having misinterpreted an ancient book containing advice on how to defeat the boss troll, Ernest attempts to defeat it with "authentic Bulgarian miak" during an interrupted school dance. The liquid proves ineffectual. However, the local children, under Ernest's tutelage, understand that the only fucking thing that makes sense when presented the clue "MI_K" is *milk*, and so begin to fight the now sizable troll army with various weapons full of the lactational substance. But at the climactic moment, the boss troll acquires an extra jolt of demon power and the milk loses its anti-troll properties. Finally, Ernest realizes the ultimate salve for the small town's troll problem: unconditional love. After dancing with the troll, calling it cute, and kissing it on the mouth, love works as an explosive agent, combusting the troll's head and dissolving his body into mush. Ernest is reunited with his pet dog, and all the actors deposit their checks.

Maybe the realism of *Ernest Scared Stupid*'s awful troll prosthetics is what terrified me as a kid. Or maybe I was fearful of its ominous linkage to my life—the protagonist child is named Kenny ("Um, that's *my* name …") and the movie's action takes place in Taylor County ("Oh man, and that's where I *live!*"), but watching it now killed the force of its scares. I was instead left to wonder at the weird cultural bubble that my generation grew up in.

Ernest Scared Stupid is emblematic of what I'll call American booger culture, an odd cultural archipelago formed in the mid 80's and lasting for a little over a decade. *Ernest Scared Stupid* came out in 1991, the same year Nickelodeon released their incredible slate of original animated series, including *Doug*, *Rugrats*, and *The Ren & Stimpy Show* (listed in ascending order of grotesqueness). Nickelodeon followed those with a block of real-life programming including *Are You Afraid of the Dark?*, *Clarissa Explains It All*, *All That*, *The Amanda Show*, and *Kenan & Kel*, four of which relied on gross-out props and parents nervous at an collective, oncoming filth. All of these programs were sandwiched between splatter-happy game shows like *Nickelodeon Guts*, *Legends of the Hidden Temple*, and *Double Dare*, the latter spawning the whole slate's spirit's most iconic consumer product: a neon, goopy, and malleable children's toy called Gak.

I was a child of these programming blocks. I was a child of Nickelodeon, Hot Pockets, and of after-school Cup Noodles ramen in front of the television, and I was a child offered up my likeness to help sell those products to other children. And I can say—from both sides—that the predominant joy of children's television in the mid-90's was getting folks dirty and grossing people out.

•

EarthBound's marketing campaign hinged on this assumption. Given a reported two million dollar marketing push by Nintendo of America, the campaign appeared in magazines and on televisions in a big way. Nintendo executives thought that *EarthBound* had the potential to sell three million copies. In hindsight, *EarthBound's* print ad campaign seems to be the canary in the coalmine for the game's failure to take off in America, featuring easily misconstrued slogans like, "It's like living inside your gym shoes." and "Because this game stinks." Instead of emphasizing *EarthBound's* crazily imaginative levels or the fact that its heroes are American kids—just like you!—the campaign urged parents to buy their kids a game via genuinely distasteful olfactory assault (i.e. the scratch-and-sniff cards).

Another commonly cited reason for consumers' tepid response to *EarthBound* is its divergent style. At the time, roleplaying games were set in the territory of fantasy or sci-fi—think swords, dragons, magic, mech warriors, and laser guns—and each game also pushed the Super Nintendo's graphical capabilities, angling to woo kids with their visual novelty, whereas *EarthBound* was markedly simple (and domestic) by design.

But even more so than its off-kilter print campaign, *EarthBound* was harmed by its physical presentation. *EarthBound*'s SNES cartridges were sold in an oversized box custom built to fit the accompanying magazine-sized *EarthBound Player's Guide*, and because of this overlarge box, *EarthBound* was often relegated to the bottom shelf of video game displays. All of these special marketing efforts tallied up to a $70 list price, about $10 costlier than most SNES games (and about $107 in 2013 money).

Like so many other masterpieces, *EarthBound* was at first considered unwieldy, then doomed to fail, and (temporarily) forgotten.

Fewer than two hundred thousand copies of *EarthBound* were sold in the US.

Out of sight, out of mind.

•

Ness and Paula are united with Jeff after he crashes his father's Sky Runner into their underground chamber. Within an hour or so, the three of you enact a plan to trap all of Threed's zombies in its central circus tent. To do so, you must first head south and fight a fanged, aggressive circus tent, but with your newfound friend Jeff constantly barraging it with bottle rockets and homemade bombs, it's an easy fight. You set the bait, watch the zombies pile into their trap, then you're off.

The next segment of the game features *EarthBound*'s most famous species: the Mr. Saturn.

The Mr. Saturn are pink, big-nosed bipeds who look like they were designed top-down to end up as *EarthBound*'s purchasable plush doll. Their native tongue pops with exclamations of "BOING!" and "ZOOM!", and is rendered onscreen in a font inspired by the handwriting of Shigesato Itoi's young daughter. They've become the Mother series' goofy, harmless mascot.

Mr. Saturn and his identical ilk have drawn comparisons to the Tralfamadorians from Kurt Vonnegut's books. But unlike those goofy alien captors that imprison Billy Pilgrim in a zoo in *Slaughterhouse-Five*, the Mr. Saturn's have been forced into slave labor by the massive, bowel-ejected overlord himself: Master Belch.

To infiltrate Belch's factory, you must first learn the password (easy enough) and also learn something much more elusive: something called *patience*. Scott and I struck our heads over and over again with our controllers and threw them against the TV screen while we tried to figure out how to get in the damn factory door.

Luckily, the *EarthBound Player's Guide* tipped us off: You have to stand in front of the door—which is obscured by the early-era video game style waterfalls—and *not touch a single button for three minutes*.

I can understand how humans landed on the moon, but I cannot understand how anyone figured this out on their own.

•

To me, the most enduringly beautiful parts of *EarthBound*—and most indicative of the wistful, philosophical aesthetic Shigesato Itoi has cultivated since he stopped making games—are its three most reflective moments. You get a chance to experience the first after you've defeated Belch and washed yourself off in a milky pink hot spring. After you've dried off, a Mr. Saturn offers you a coffee. Who are you to say no?

After a beat, a blue-green lava lamp pattern fills the screen, and hypnotic little amoebas rhythmically con-tract and divide and rise beyond you as this text scrolls up:

> "You've traveled very far from home … Do you remember how your long and winding journey began with someone pounding at your door? It was Pokey, the worst person in your neighborhood, who knocked on the door that fateful night. On your way, you have walked, thought and fought. Yet through all this, you have never lost your courage. You have grown steadily stronger, though you have experienced the pain of battle many times. You are no longer alone in your adventure, Paula who is steadfast, kind and even pretty, is always at your side. Jeff is with you as well. Though he is timid, he came from a distant land to help you. Ness, as you certainly know by now, you are not a regular young man … You have an awesome destiny to fulfill. The journey from this point will be long, and it will be more difficult than anything you have undergone to this point. Yet, I know you will be all right. When good battles evil, which side do you believe wins? Do you have faith that good is triumphant? One thing you must never lose is courage. If you believe in the goal you are striving for, you will be courageous. There are many dif-

ficult times ahead, but you must keep your sense of humor, work through the tough situations and enjoy yourself. When you have finished this cup of coffee, your adventure will begin again. Next, you must pass through a vast desert and proceed to the big city of Fourside. Ness … Paula … Jeff … I wish you luck …"

•

Other than serving as a narrative recap and a basic philosophical inquiry, this coffee break feels like a pep talk. And a pep talk like the one I got from my dad when I came home from my first pilot season without having booked any work.

It's hard to describe my dad, but my wife calls him "the real life Marlboro Man." During most of my childhood, I remember him wearing his mechanic workman's blue uniform and a thick mustache, a cigarette constantly fixed between his lips (he has smoked about a pack a day of Camel Regulars since he was fourteen). He used to race top-fuel motorcycles on the 1/8th mile, and one accident in the pits left him with a charred, chewed-up right leg that has since turned a necrotic brown from the knee down and that refuses to bend. He's got an artificial heart valve that clicks out a comforting clockwork, and his hands are so arthritic his joints and knuckles look like crudely drawn exercises by a childish draftsman. His use of profanities to communicate—have you seen *A Christmas Story*? Remember the dad's string of curse words while futzing around with the boiler? My dad's deployment of colorful language is like that but *times a thousand*, and constant—and it's legendary among my family and friends, as is his hatred of condiments of any sort. (I've seen hamburgers almost evaporate due to the force of their impact against our living room window.) I've also seen him fix people's cars even though they couldn't yet pay him to. I've seen him cry for hours before putting down a stray cat that convulsed with rabies. I've seen how openly haunted he was made by burying one of our dogs who had been run over by a truck just after dawn. And I've seen him cry, bedridden, while saying goodbye to us before his open-heart surgery.

I remember sitting on the edge of the bed in my parents' bedroom and breathing in the soaked-in nicotine smell kept in the room's fabric while my dad said stuff that would be at home in any of the Good Dad speeches crystallized by Hollywood screenwriters: That if I kept trying, I'd get what I wanted. That I just had to work hard. That I had to "prove all those motherfucking cocksucking assholes who didn't pick you *wrong*." (Well, I haven't heard that one in the movies.) And that he and mom would support me all the way.

The next year, my mom, my little sister and I returned to Los Angeles while my dad staid in Potosi and fixed cars. For six months at a time, and then eight months, and then a year, and then another year, and one more year, just like Ness and his father, I only heard my dad's voice over the phone.

FOURSIDE

Now, THE MORE I write about *EarthBound*, the less I want to play it.

To say this more clearly: The more I examine *Earth-Bound*, the more I want to examine it. The more I want to keep using it as a portal, as a lever by which I can lift my childhood and the bacterial growth of my aesthetic tastes into a better, truer light.

Or maybe it's only that the game is getting harder.

•

Before progressing to Fourside, *EarthBound*'s metropolis, you're forced to explore a vast, sun-beaten desert. Well, when I say vast, I'm talking Super Nintendo vast here. Vast enough to require a methodical, gridded exploration if you don't want to miss anything. The dusty map's size, though, is *nothing* compared to those of RPGs and massively multiplayer online role-playing games created since. *World of Warcraft* is made up of eighty square miles. *Just Cause 2*, one of the sandbox-style games I played last year, contains four hundred square miles of explorable, digital terrain. But the largest game map, by leagues—by crushing, mind-snuffing leaps and bounds—belongs to *Elder Scrolls II: Daggerfall*. Released in 1996 on MS-DOS, Daggerfall presents sixty-two *thousand*, three hundred and ninety-four square miles for your play and perusal, an area a little larger and a lot more dimensionally boring than Georgia and that is dotted with more than seven hundred and fifty thousand NPCs to interact with, albeit repetitively.

You explore the Dusty Dunes Desert on foot, battling scorpions, exploding orbs, and heatstroke. You quickly stumble upon your next goal: Find a hungry gold miner and give him some food.

Before heading into Dusty Dunes, I consulted Starmen.net's *EarthBound* walkthrough, vaguely remembering a challenging set of dungeons in this part of the map. Sure enough, the walkthrough confirmed this, and recommended I stock up on food and herbs. With a great sense of diligence, I began to backtrack, preparing for the upcoming challenges in the ways deemed most effective by my Starmen.net guides.

Rarely in the realm of the flesh have I been as prepared as I am in almost all video games: I obsessively check drawers, pilfer medicine cabinets, steal supplies, craft items and load up at the shop. I'm diligent with money, but also am keenly sensitive for a good deal, ambiently aware of fair market price in a video game as much as I am of the temperature in real life. My inventories are clean, ordered, cautiously spacious, and always a source of anxiety. In a word, I play video games like obsessive-compulsives organize their homes.

But I'm a terrible survivalist. I don't know how to start a fire by spinning sticks. I can't set a broken bone. I can't identify the North Star, or sniff out potable water or edible berries. To me, dead reckoning sounds like a Western movie. I've used a Swiss Army knife exactly twice, and have accidentally stabbed myself in the hand with a Swiss Army knife exactly twice. For all the shit talk I spew about being the guy to stick with when the zombie apocalypse occurs, if I'm being honest, you might want to find someone who's at least an Eagle Scout. Preferably some large, muscled guy (maybe a Brad) who has drunk his own pee while free climbing a local mountain. A guy who owns multiple pairs of variously cleated shoes. A woman who has served in the military, given birth, or who uses her body in a fitnessy way. Someone who has camped *once*.

But if you need someone to get you through a tough little boss fight, call me.

•

When I was fourteen, my mom, little sister, and I lived in a 400 square feet partially furnished studio in the Oakwood Toluca Hills corporate apartment complex in Burbank, California.

The Oakwood is notorious in Hollywood for housing about 400 families per year that have moved to Los Angeles to help—or, if they fully embody the stage parent cliché, force—their children to find acting work. The Oakwood has been the subject to a lot of media coverage because of this annual influx of ostentatious kids attempting to join the rank of Oakwood residents who went on to work—e.g. Jennifer Love Hewitt, Hilary Duff, Demi Lovato, Frankie Muniz, Kirsten Dunst, and Fred Savage—and the Oakwood corporate brass caters to this rush, offering "Child Actor Rates" for renting one of their apartments through January and March (pilot season) or August and December (episodic season). According to their 2014 pricing, the same studio apartment that my family and I lived in now costs $2,370 per month.

But the high costs weren't only financial. When I stayed at the Oakwood, I had the nightly opportunity to drink booze, smoke weed, and gamble (and tried to spin these opportunities into a nightly opportunity to have sex), all of which are totally permissible activities for adults but iffy for twelve-to-sixteen year olds. The clubhouse grounds were marked by wafted coughs of pot smoke, the clatter of clay chips, and an infamously *fluid*-filled hot tub. My mom knew about all this but held the line of encouraging me to be responsible, or at least honest when I hadn't been. A little drinking and past-curfew property damage aside, I was a good egg, spurred to play it safe by Scott's spectacularly hungover (like crawling-down-a-flight-of-stairs-on-his-hands-and-knees-hungover) mornings. Many of my friends quickly lost their desire to act (and therefore to support themselves), and then lost their desire to do anything other than drink, smoke, gamble, and fuck. Oakwood was like a 1/60th scale *Deadwood*, but murder was much rarer, and there were golf carts.

•

Not long after becoming known as Japan's hippest adman, Shigesato Itoi became a bonafide celebrity, morphing from a copywriter to a well-known author, host, and performer. Between appearing on *Iron Chef*, performing in films like the 2010 film adaptation of Haruki Murakami's book *Norwegian Wood*, lending his voice to Studio Ghibli's animated films, and writing uncategorizable books that contain essays, interviews, and fiction, Itoi has transcended any specific label, having attained the hard-to-attain fame for being a *tastemaker*. And that's not even considering his largest project to date.

For the past fifteen years, Itoi has been the editor-in-chief and a daily writer for Hobo Nikkan Itoi Shimbun (translation: Almost-Daily Itoi Newspaper). From a recent *Japan Times* profile of Itoi:

"Despite his use of the word *shimbun* (newspaper) in the title of his media organ"—I want to invite you real quick to join me in my love of the phrase *media organ*— "Itoi's version is far removed from conventional newspapers at the basic level of it not carrying news reports per se. Nor does it rely on wire services such as Kyodo, AP, Reuters or whatever."

Itoi's online-only site has featured a wide range of material, including moderated discussions with science professors, gardeners, local eccentrics, and former Prime Ministers, as well as reader-submitted stories about their children. With Hobonichi, as it's known, Itoi has created a laid-back and anti-sensationalist newspaper that doesn't ignore the involvement of its founder; Itoi muses daily on philosophy and poetry alongside photographs of his dog Bouillon.

This perpetual and amorphous venture has been incredibly successful. Hobonichi does not carry any advertising, instead relying sales of Hobonichi-branded products—like towels, t-shirts, daily planners—to finance itself. So far, so good: The site brings in more than one million page views every day, and in 2011 Itoi's company posted the equivalent of $28,694,400 in sales, netting $3,074,400.

One of the endeavor's bestselling products, the Hobonichi Techo, is a gorgeous daily planner replete with a gold-stamped leather cover, pleasing fonts, and considerate design. Each two-day spread subtly features a quote acquired from one of Hobonichi's interviews, essays or articles, each philosophical by nature. There's one in particular that caught me: it's framed as a lone square .jpg on the 2013 planner's English language page. I won't attribute it, as it's more beautiful apart from its source:

My own death, the deaths of my friends,
the killing of others, and the killing of others' friends:
on August 15, I'm reminded that all these are equally sad.

Am I wrong?

•

After shortcutting around the Dusty Dunes traffic jam, you wind up in Fourside.

To start, the size of the city's buildings strains *EarthBound*'s oblique projection system (a 3D scheme familiar to anyone who has played the arcade and NES game *Paperboy*, a game that, in the arcade version, used a digital chip called POKEY to render its sound). And while Fourside is *EarthBound*'s most populous and moneyed city, I couldn't help but notice the hair color of all its administrators. At one point, while seeing The Runaway Five in the Toppola Theater, you're surrounded by an audience composed *entirely* by blondes. So, like the cities in so many video games, Fourside is large but not at all cosmopolitan.

Fourside's got some charmingly honest denizens, though. When you approach a middle-aged woman (blonde) circling the interior of Fourside's bakery, she says: "Bread in this town has a very plain, nondescript flavor to it. To tell you the truth, I'm the owner of this bakery."

The odious events in Fourside are prophetic of the American mortgage crisis of 2008: Fourside's mayor, Geldegarde Monotoli, has been driven mad with power and is evicting people from their homes and businesses to take over their real estate while simultaneously bending the police force to protect him instead of Fourside's residents. Playing through the city now, I wish for an Occupy Fourside movement to take Monotoli and his new adviser Pokey Minch—a precursor to *South Park*'s rotund, blond instigator Eric Cartman—to task.

•

The next event in the game serves as a sort of schism. There's pre-Moonside *EarthBound* and there's post-Moonside *EarthBound*. Pre-Moonside *Earth-Bound* presents a trope-reliant quirkiness, whereas post-Moonside *EarthBound* fractals out into an increasingly metaphysical, violent, and weird series of realms and challenges.

Moonside, simply put, is where shit gets crazy.

Fourside's Cafe is already marked with funky music and funkier patrons. A quick visit there leads to an encounter in the alleyway with your old criminal pal Everdred, who lays fatally wounded on the pavement. He expalins: Monotoli tricked him out of the Evil Mani Mani statue, the mind-bending MacGuffin that warps its users into power-hungry assholes (including the leader of all those Happy Happyists). This thing's a hot commodity, and it's got its corrosive claws in Fourside's mayor. The dying Everdred encourages you to confront its power, but to do so, you've got to start by checking behind the bar in Jackie's Cafe.

You walk inside, then walk behind the bar, face the wall, and examine it.

Nothing.

You look harder, searching its panels, its texture. You examine it.

Nothing.

You walk away for a second but then return, sure you already looked at this one particular spot—

???

•

If Dadaism, waterlogged funhouse music, neon lighting, and creepy black velvet paintings all fucked and had a child, it would be Moonside.

Moonside, the bent nightmare version of Fourside, is a space marked by its eschewed logic—yes means no, no means yes—and its warped layout. In a particularly frustrating inverse, Fourside's infrastructure and implements of wealth—property, cabs, fire hydrants, abstract art—are now vicious enemies. (Scott and I died over and over again in fights with one of Dali's melting clocks. And got lost among the teleportation-enabled surfer bros that are Moonside's sole mode of transportation. And spent *hours* looking for the invisible man with a unibrow and a gold tooth.) Unless you've spent hours leveling up your party, Moonside is *hard*. It's hard in a way that no section of *EarthBound* has been before. Instead of charging into fights, you strategically dodge them, or run away, or try to edge the enemies out of existence.

What do I mean by edging? (Well, what is the nonsexual connotation of the word?) *EarthBound*'s enemies are randomly generated, so if you find an up-coming area filled with baddies you'd rather avoid, you can walk away and then come back to a hopefully less threatening number of on-screen enemies.

Game designer Michel McBride-Charpentier beautifully notices: "It recently occurred to me that my little maneuvers used to exploit a "bug" reflected the hesitation Ness must feel. A few steps forward, run away, gather courage, approach again, and yes, it turns out the enemies weren't so bad after all. We can both go on."

•

You defeat the Mani Mani statue and wake up in a warehouse, the statue crushed to pieces in front of you. *EarthBound*'s occasional omniscient narrator delivers some exposition about the Mani Mani statue's power to create illusions, including Moonside. Finished with the hallucinogenic, absurdist gauntlet, you are free to walk back into the world of weak-willed plutocrats and Euclidean navigation. Fourside's daylight is sobering.

But you quickly go back into wackiness. Your next task is to wind your way through a series of caverns in the Dusty Dunes Desert, strategically bribing talkative monkeys with hamburgers, pizzas, and other food-stuffs to let you deeper into the maze. After Moonside, this portion of the game feels easy; after escaping the threat of sunstroke, you might feel the relief of this underground chamber's cooler air. Your reward for these labyrinthine acts of bribery: A levitating time-space continuum guru has his monkeys teach you how to teleport.

The monkey maze seems stressless, but not for the completist who wants to ferret out its rare items. Without the Nintendo *Player's Guide*, Scott and I might've quit playing *EarthBound* at this point. Scott was easily frustrated back then, but also obsessive—he played games and coded programs for sixteen hours straight, hid drug stashes with a spider-like speed and meticulousness, and taught himself elaborate guitar solos by ear and uninhibited will. I remember admiring his lack of fear in the face of a challenge. So, monkey see monkey do: When Scott got frustrated, I aped his frustration. And when he decided to *swing* back into *EarthBound*, I joined him.

After rescuing Paula from Monotoli, she receives a psychic urge to travel to the city of Summers. Monotoli offers to lend you his private helicopter, but Pokey steals the craft, taunts you, and then runs away.

After a brief trip to Threed to fix up the Sky Runner, you are whisked across Itoi's purple sky.

•

After four years of living in Los Angeles in cramped apartments with my mom and little sister, and after four years of the three of us seeing dad fewer than three weeks a year, and after landing the veritable lottery by booking a starring role in pilot four times only to be told each time—after months of the anticipation and hair-graying anxiety and emotional rollercoastering incurred by following by the industry-wide TV rumor mill—that all four pilots would *not* be picked up to series; after the tens of thousands of miles of driving to and from auditions and callbacks and screen tests and network tests—most of which taking place in austere conference rooms or Lynchian theaters filled with straight-lipped and/or yawning suits—and after four years of inhabiting but resisting the actor's perpetual fog of unknowing—*did that audition go well?*—and of unknowableness—*why didn't I book that part?*—I finally booked a lead role in a TV series that was guaranteed to have ten episodes produced and aired on national television.

The ink was dry, and my call time was 6:00 AM sharp.

Step out on that balcony, folks.

You're in Summers now.

SUMMERS

SUMMERS IS $49 gelato.

•

Nassim Nicholas Taleb: "The three most harmful addictions are heroin, carbohydrates, and a monthly salary."

•

I began making around $500,000 per year when I was eighteen.

When you've just reached the age in which the United States legally sanctions you to murder people, the obvious benefits of making enormous sums of money are many. The most important and bulletproof benefits being: You can afford good health insurance. You can live in a neighborhood of your choice. You can afford food that won't slowly poison you. The less clear-cut benefits: You can afford to drive almost any car (which also means you can have an 1800 lb., fiberglass-bodied racecar custom built for you that would nine-times-out-of-ten murder you dead during a medium-sized collision). You can live in a nice house (which also means you can incur a mortgage of $450,000—or about $2,500 per month—just months after moving out of Mom's place). You can frequently dine in your city's finest restaurants (which also means you can indulge your inner glutton to paroxysms of binge eating, thereby activating your unknown but latent case of Crohn's disease thereby hospitalizing you for a near-fatal abscess formed by a leaking hole in your intestines). And you can buy a bunch of fancy shit.

I starred in an hour-long cable TV show, and my salary was kind of earned in that I showed up on time and performed the services asked of me—laugh, cry, fret, empathize, rage, charm, appease, and mull, all the while saying the scripted lines of dialogue while hitting my marks—but not really earned in that we—"we" meaning television actors with series regular contracts—are paid *way too fucking much*. And a television program's showrunners (the leading writer/producers) are paid exponentially more.

The palace of televised entertainment is gilded with millions of eyes and monthly cable-bundle charges.

•

Because my parents aren't sociopaths, I was raised to be kind to strangers. This habit—made up by transactional microbursts of deference enacted hundreds of times per day while moving through a large city—is the first thing to go when a person becomes rich.

After my wife and I got engaged, we went to Europe. We spent time with friends who were living modestly in Paris and Rome, and we spent time in fancy hotels because I argued that it was necessary to "see how the 1% live." I was raised to feel like an impostor among the rich because my family was middle class and they therefore healthily distrusted the wealthy. So while I claimed a higher motive to spend time and money in fancy hotels and restaurants, I was lying to myself. I wanted some luxury and my culture said honeymoons or engagement trips were a time to take it.

One incident in particular cemented the belief that I don't belong in that world. We were staying at the Ritz Hotel in Paris for two nights, and we wanted to take a taxi across town to dinner. We walked outside and stood by the only other couple waiting for a cab: he was balding, portly and starched; she was young, tall, and gorgeous. With senses either animalistic, cultural, or both, I sniffed this guy's fucking attitude. But I hoped he'd prove me wrong. The Parisian porter was trying to hail some cabs with a silver whistle, but no drivers in the nearby flock could work during their mandatory breaks. From behind me, I heard the white-shirt's first scoff. I ignored it, and caught the porter's eye to ask—as politely as I knew how, hoping to offset the constant abuse he surely had to deal with—for a cab headed south. We had reservations for dinner and we'd probably be late, but it was our fault. And then behind us: a second scoff. I turned my head and stared at the guy. He looked at his Rolex and mumbled, "Fucking ridiculous." I kept staring. My wife squeezed my hand, aware that this kind of stuff bends me close to violence. We waited. A few silent minutes in Paris's most moneyed square. The porter approached us and apologized for the lack of cabs and I shrugged it off. Starched Prick was now constantly muttering. Loudly. He started shouting at the porter in clipped, whiny ejections, the kind that come from a creature ossified into a sort of immovable fuckwad exoskeleton by years of money and privilege. Aviva was crushing my hand by now, and the porter ignored the guy. Finally, a cab glided in front of the hotel. The white-shirt started to walk towards it, but the porter jumped off the curb, opened the back door, and gestured to my wife: "After you, madame." Aviva turned to him, beaming, and I smiled at the guy and passed him some Euros and got in the car. As our cab rolled away, I caught the white-shirt standing there stupefied by the kids in jeans and sneakers.

•

I like to spin that story, angling its moral to read: Do not be an asshole among assholes and you will get places. But nobody will ever purely know the porter's motivation, or the asshole's financial situation, or the depth of his relationship with his companion. Rich humans are humans still, but they're humans who can freely use the most powerful tool in human history: a surplus of money. Tools impartially magnify our powers, which means they magnify our cruelty just as well as our magnanimity. So it's foolish to characterize the rich as inhuman, or as monsters, because that casts them as intrinsically bad or incapable of humanity instead of what they are: an opportunistic animal that is easily bent by the resources available to it, like all of us. And like most members of every small group throughout history with access to something they deem vital to their existence, they want to protect it. Because the human animal's sense of territory is so overbearing, a sort of overinflated self-protecting balloon forms around him. This balloon, to its wearer, feels like virtue. It feels like license. It feels like being chosen.

As someone who received the tool of wealth without any obligation to use it to do good (i.e. help people in dire need), I can verify that it's much easier to misuse. Entire industries rely on that misuse. And it's easy to feel like you have to wear that protective air to not get taken advantage of. It's easy to become Starched Prick.

•

Playing through Summers, then, is hitting me all in all sorts of familiar and sensitive places. Overpriced jewelry, pandering service professionals, spoiled tourists, haughty haute hotties … Summers has it all.

Styled after a resort town like Cannes or Nice, Summers quickly becomes the source of my favorite lines in the game. I took so many photos of my screen. Some favorites include:

From a supine male sunbather, one arm up as if holding an invisible tray: "Only a tanning pro like me is able to get an actual suntan on the palms of his hands!"

From a waitress in a fancy restaurant: "[Insert your favorite food here. My choice: Carbs]? Please ... we do not have such trash on our menu."

And, in the exclusive Stoic Club, one of its armchair philosophers speaks my favorite line in any video game ever: "You guys can't envision the final collapse of capitalism? Incredible!"

•

The Stoic Club, in its emphasis on philosophical conversation, is basically a parody of the Great Books college I'm about to leave Hollywood for, so it is killing me in a good way.

And the placement of the club in Summers suggests that the dangers of wealth are similar to the dangers of academic knowledge. Both can be mistaken as a sign that their possessor has access to some higher reality, be it the movement of the markets or the music of the spheres.

So *EarthBound* is instructing me how not to think and speak during the next four years.

•

But what Ness, Paula, and Jeff are *really* looking for in the Stoic Club is not philosophy but a magic slice of cake.

See, to progress past this whitewashed resort town, you need to hop on a boat. But the only sea captain in town willing to give you a ride is in a bad way with his wife, and you've been tasked to find her in the Stoic Club and patch up their marital relations. To do this, though, you must eat her homemade hallucinogenic cake.

After devouring your slice on the edge of the beach, the town and its sand warp into a nauseating purple and pink phosphenic trip.

•

Scared by my friend's burnouts in Los Angeles and Scott's abysmal hangovers, I didn't smoke weed until I was eighteen, somehow thinking that it too would commit forest fires.

I was in Louisiana working on a movie that shall go unnamed. When I tell people about this movie, I say that no matter how many bare breasts were captured jiggling by thousands of feet of 35mm film stock, the film *wasn't* softcore porn, but it *should've* been, because it would've been more honest that way. It was an independent film that had a budget of more than fifteen-million dollars, a significant portion of which were spent on fireworks, jet skis, scooters, plastic pools filled with Jell-O, busing in attractive background actors from nearby college towns to dance around in bikinis, and about a thousand pies that were all deployed in a massive, illegibly-filmed pie fight. The film was shut down by multiple unions multiple times.

The town was small and the shoot was chaotic in every way imaginable, so its actors and its crew did what any sane group of people with per diem would do: drugs. Every night, the cast and crew drank the *entire hotel bar*. Weed was everywhere, and a fellow actor was a proselytizer: His inspired sermon about the astounding genetic varieties of marijuana strains was enough to send me over the edge. We sat in the fellow actor's hotel room, put on the movie *Army of Darkness*, and proceeded to smoke weed. Cursed with a high tolerance for second-hand smoke because of my dad's cigarettes, I was able to inhale chiefly hits. And like most first-time smokers, I didn't feel anything for about fifteen minutes, so I kept smoking.

And then I became aware of how *Army of Darkness*'s crew set up *every single one* of the movie's shots.

The rest of the night is a blur. I remember playing an arcade version of *NFL Blitz* but then quitting, unable to remember which of the two buttons was Run and which was Tackle.

I remember taking a bite of a Duchess Honey Bun and dropping to my knees, screaming, "I CAN TASTE EVERY INGREDIENT!"

And, unfortunately, I remember feeling parched. To quench my thirst, I grabbed the nearest bottle of water and drank down huge gulps. Roughly thirty seconds later, I realized I had just swallowed roughly sixteen fluid ounces of bong-water.

I smoked weed three or four more times since, and I proved unable to go a few stoned hours without humiliating myself as much as I did during that virginal first high, so four or five years ago, I quit the drug for good.

•

After eating the slice of magic cake, you drift to a floating land impossibly nested in the clouds, and suddenly you're in control of Poo, the teenaged Crown Prince of the mystical kingdom of Dalaam.

Remember when I said that shit gets crazy after Moonside?

Prepare yourself.

•

Your first mission as Poo is to bring him into spiritual maturity. Poo's master instructs him to go to the place of emptiness to endure his final trial.

After winding your way down the tiered slopes of your floating kingdom (and shrugging off the affections of Dalaam's ladies), you reach the base of a multilevel pillar of land. A sign reads:

"This is Mu, the place of nothingness. People who train here must first clear everything from their minds. If you can make your mind blank and learn the true meaning of Mu you'll pass through. Mu is Mu ..."

Mu is many, many things:

Mu is the Nasdaq stock ticker for Micron Technology, Inc., an American multinational corporation based in Boise, Idaho that produces semiconductors.

Mu is the fictional continent lost to the seas at the dawn of human history. The idea of Mu was first proposed by Augustus Le Plongeon, a photographer and antiquarian who studied the ruins of the Maya civilization. Augustus got the name from Charles Étienne Brasseur de Bourbourg, a 19th century specialist in Mesoamerican studies who published a flawed translation of the larger fragment of the Madrid Codex, one of three surviving Maya books dating from 900–1521 AD. Charles—using a flawed Rosetta stone of sorts called the de Landa alphabet—mistranslated the word

Mu to mean "a land submerged by a catastrophe." (Tangentially, the thick black lines and strong, simple faces of the Maya codices remind me of a lot of contemporary graphic novels—the Dresden Codex seems right at home next to the cover to *Epileptic* by David B.—which reminds me of that familiar Biblical message: "The thing that hath been, it is that which shall be; and that which is done is that which shall be done: and there is no new thing under the sun.")

Mu is also the 12th letter of the Greek alphabet. As a symbol, mu has uses in a wide variety of disciplines, from mathematics to music to meat science. And in the system of Greek numerals, Mu has a value of 40.

In Douglas Adam's book *The Hitchhiker's Guide to the Galaxy*, a group of pan-dimensional beings build a supercomputer—dubbed Deep Thought—that is meant to formulate the Answer to the Ultimate Question of Life, The Universe, and Everything. After 7,500,000 years of computation, Deep Thought reveals the answer: 42.

With Mu, we've been tantalizingly robbed of a poetic Question to match Deep Thought's Answer (by just two digits): Mu is the word most commonly used in zazen, Zen Buddhism's meditative practice, and in Japanese and Korean, *mu*—or *wu* in Chinese—means "not have; without."

In the classic book of Zen koans, *The Gateless Gate,* the first case reads:

A monk asked Jōshū, "Has a dog the Buddha Nature?" Jōshū answered, "Mu."

•

Or: What is the Answer to the Ultimate Question of Life, The Universe, and Everything?

42.

Then what is the Ultimate Question of Life, The Universe, and Everything?

Nothing.

•

I discovered Zen Buddhism when I was sixteen, reading online about Buddhism's origins, its purpose (and purposelessness), its schools and intimations and practices. I was hooked. That day I began to meditate. I started off slowly, only dipping my toes into self-silence for ten or twenty minutes at a time. But within a few months, I could sit still with my eyes closed for hours, feeling spiritually aligned and in touch with my newfound calling. How serious was I? Well, when I wasn't Photoshopping lens flares and wind effects into pictures of myself in various Buddhist poses—hoping to lose my virginity to a lady (ideally *ladies*) who found me super-enlightened and stuff—I almost enlisted in a three-month-long Buddhist retreat in Los Angeles. I was drawn to the idea of chop wood, carry water, which is best evinced by this koan:

A monk told Jōshū, "I have just entered the monastery. Please teach me." Jōshū asked, "Have you eaten your rice porridge? The monk replied, "I have eaten." Jōshū said, "Then you had better wash your bowl." At that moment the monk was enlightened.

The simplicity and practical progression of that life was appealing to me then and is even more appealing now. How the hyperconnected itch for a calmer mind and the coziness of limited possibilities only grows.

Eventually though, my overwhelming teenage desires didn't square with Buddhism's simple contentedness, and my childhood allergy to religion flared back up to expel it. But zazen—and thinking *mu, mu, mu*—made a small but indelible mark on my life.

•

The Google query as the modern path to enlightenment.

•

According to the *EarthBound* wiki, Poo is older than Ness, making him approximately seventeen years old.

Jōshū, one of the greatest Chinese Zen masters, describes his first experience of Buddhist insight, also at age seventeen: "Suddenly I was ruined and homeless."

•

You, as Poo, climb up three ropes to your barren patch of dirt. Like Simeon Stylites, the Christian canonized for his extremely ascetic acts, you sit atop this pillar, eyes closed, legs crossed, and meditate on Mu.

Dalaam's exotic, chipper soundtrack is replaced by a throaty drone that sounds like a swarm of high-powered spiritual vehicles barreling towards you. This loops, and loops, and loops.

Time passes.

A messenger from your master approaches, shouting up to you that your master orders you to stop your meditation immediately, much like the desert Elders who, wanting to see if Simeon's extreme acts were founded in humility or pride, commanded him to come down off his pillar, planning to leave him be if he proved obedient. Simeon proved obedient, and, having done the right thing, he was left atop his pillar for thirty-seven years. You, as Poo, however, ignore the messenger. You don't move. You maintain mu, maintain the drone.

Then: black.

•

A light static.

A ghostlike head drifts down over you. A spirit of your ancient lineage. It intones:

To complete your trial, I am going to break your legs. You will lose the use of them. Do you accept this?

Wait. What do you do here? The correct answer must not be *no*. So …

Yes, you accept this. A catastrophic sound—your health begins to drain away.

So, Prince Poo … you cannot walk, as your legs are broken. Next, I will tear your arms off. I shall then take your arms and feed them to the crows. The taking of your arms … Do you accept this?

Yes, you accept this. A deeper, deadlier sound—your life now emptied. You are either unconscious or dead.

Ahh, Prince Poo ... without legs and arms, you can only lie there ... Now, I'll cut your ears off. You do not mind my taking your hearing away, do you? Do you accept this?

Yes, you accept this. A quick ripping sound—then silence. The drone gone.

You hear nothing.

So, Prince Poo. No legs, no arms and no sound. By floating words through the air, I must ask you ... Do you care if I take your eyes? Do you want to live in eternal darkness? I shall steal your sight ... Do you accept this?

Yes, you accept this.

Black.

So, Prince Poo. Now I can only communicate directly with your mind. Your mind is all you have left. In the end, I will take your mind, though you probably don't want to allow that, do you. So ... you can't answer? You can't even move? Are you sad, are you lonely? If you lose your mind, you also lose any feelings of sadness ... Do you accept this? I will take your mind, Prince Poo, know that I will possess it ...

Within seconds, you're on your feet, Dalaam's music returns, and you're notified that you've completed your training.

•

In a piece of popular children's entertainment, you're encouraged to submit to the severance of limbs and of sense in pursuit of spiritual enlightenment. It's a terminal mythical challenge, and there's no way around it. If you press a button on the controller or reject any of the spirit's propositions, you must retrace your steps, return to the palace, and talk to your master, who then sends you to start all over again.

I can't truly know how deeply *EarthBound* affected me as a kid, or how responsible it is for shaping my philosophy or my aesthetics (i.e. being attracted to art that other people describe as difficult, confusing, brutal, or just batshit crazy). But I do know that this is a disturbing challenge to require a young kid to face, and it felt even more disturbing to face as an adult.

•

Interestingly enough, all of the Mu training dialogue is absent from the *EarthBound* scripts available online.

•

I've taken to playing *EarthBound* late at night, sitting in an armchair with the Starmen.net walkthrough loaded on my iPhone for easy reference. I've been playing for three or four hours per sit, trying to mainline the game's narrative by speeding through *EarthBound*'s actual "game" mechanics (fighting enemies, buying stuff, navigating dungeons).

To be honest, I'm getting tired.

About three years ago, Aviva and I stayed at my mom and dad's house in Potosi, Texas during Christmas. My dad still lives in the house I grew up in, but my mom and younger sister have long since resettled in Los Angeles. Again, my mom and dad are still married, and still live physically apart from each other because of the relocation started by my career in entertainment. After my sister started going to school in L.A., my parents decided it made sense for my mom and sister to not return to Abilene. Eventually, the plan went, my dad would sell his auto repair business, their house, and their land, and then rejoin the family out west.

Seven years have passed.

That Christmas, Aviva and I slept in my old bedroom—a 10 x 9' affair with its westernmost wall painted blood red and the rest of the room full of swords, dragon figurines, and other assorted geekery—and spent most of our waking hours binge-watching two seasons of *Breaking Bad* on my laptop.

One morning, with the smell of frying bacon coming down the hall and into my old bedroom, I found in my closet a familiar looking multicolored cardboard box. I retrieved it from a dusty hollow formed by sloppy stacks of white plastic bins containing comic books and action figures. I called out into the hallway for Aviva. She came in, and I asked her to come look at my childhood with me.

We cracked open its stiff lid together, revealing a haggard collection of foreign coins and errant lucky charms, their purpose and origins long forgotten. We looked at the rocks and arrowheads recovered from our small ranch's pastures, the scraps of love letters never sent. The box was labeled KENNY'S SPECIAL STUFF.

Aviva filled the room with awwwws while I stared at the rocks I used to feel were special. These dull objects signaled the time in my life in which I was the most innocent, the most eager. I'd been so happy to imbue the inert, common masses all around me with integrity. With *magic*. I was staring at proof that my attention when I was five and six was as joyously sacral as it could ever be.

But I play *EarthBound* now and I'm tired by its scope. I'm tired by my inability to know how deeply it is a part of me. I'm tired by the amount of life I've already lived, and how much is left. And I'm tired by the fact that we seem to sleep so far away from that casual, lived-in joy because we have—by living as an adult—accrued so much evidence against its use and its possibility.

But we *can* wake and decide to grow that joy again, hoping its ease and humor will become ever-present for good this time.

Only to return to sleep, and then to dream, and then to wake with an unnameable piece of that dream that seems again impossible to wholly retrieve, and a question: Wasn't that joy just as fleeting when I was a child?

•

The game moves as I move through it, passing through its levels, its designs, its puzzles and failures and restful nights.

Ness gets homesick, and he gets tired. I understand his fatigue. But even though I feel it, I also feel the pull of the long quest, of the journey away from home. I felt it when I set out to transcend my self by pretending to be other people, and I did when I set out to transcend a small-town life that seemed dangerously boring, shortening my childhood and splintering my family for a decade in in the process. And now *again* I feel the pull, but this time towards a quieter, more meditative life. I feel the pull of contemplation in the desert. I feel the pull of a more private quest, one free of other people's attention, so gladly given to a questing hero.

EarthBound, then, is one of things left in the time before shit got complicated. And, luckily, I can (sort of) return to it. Out into all those lost days.

•

Days that so frequently felt like entire summers.

DEEP DARKNESS

AND WHAT COMES next is a sort of hell.

After conquering *EarthBound*'s Middle Eastern desert, you guide a yellow submarine—that Beatles reference explicit enough for you?—into a river that sweeps you towards the Deep Darkness, a primordial swamp of poisonous waters, usurious lenders, and the return of fightable puke piles. After slogging through this section, you enter Tenda Village, a tiny cave full of tinier members of a shy green species. How do you get them talking? Well, you've got to bring them a book called *Overcoming Shyness* that was recently spotted in the personal library of Apple Kid, the sloppy child inventor who has furnished you with MacGuffins since you met him early on in Twoson. (The rival inventor in town, Orange Kid, is preppy, well-prepared, popular, and totally incompetent, whereas Apple Kid is messy, brilliant, and actually useful.)

Apparently, though, Apple Kid has been kidnapped and stowed away in an alien base beneath Stonehenge.

And here is where the self-inflicted pain begins.

•

Before approaching this area of the game, I was reminded by the Starmen.net walkthrough that the Stonehenge Base is the home of the Starman Super, an encounterable enemy that is basically a souped up gold version of the Starman you encountered way back at the beginning of the game outside your home in Onett. The walkthrough benignly points out:

"The Sword of Kings is Poo's only weapon in the game, and this is your only chance to get it. Once you beat the boss, all the enemies will disappear. If you want to try to win this weapon, check out the strategies in the more detailed Sword of Kings Tips Page."

A memory like a blast of wind: Scott and I *worked* to get the Sword of Kings. I don't remember exactly how long it took us, but I remember it was its own quest.

I turn this memory over in my head, examining its worth, trying to dissolve its relevance to the job at hand, which is to play the rest of *EarthBound* and write about it. But I finally conclude that *no*, I can't avoid the Sword of Kings side quest because I'd knowingly avoid recreating my childhood experience of *Earth-Bound* to the fullest, which goes against the grain of the whole damned enterprise. So I click through to the boldly—and in hindsight, ominously boldly—labeled page: SWORD OF KINGS TIPS.

•

The gist is simple: you walk back and forth over a metal bridge to spawn and fight Starman Supers. There is no difference between the sprites of the Starman—also present in the level—and the Starman Super, though. You want to avoid the other enemy, the Atomic Power Robot, because he/she/it explodes when defeated, damaging up to three of your heroes and generally being a pain in the ass. The only other thing you must remember is how to approach the Starman Super (and the regular old Starman): Each moves via teleportation, fuzzing out and reappearing about ¼ of a screen's width away, so the best way to approach them is from the sides, where they're weirdly blind. And if you time the approach just right and make sure that you bait one Starman at a time so as to avoid mandatorily fighting multiple enemies at once, you'll merit a surprise attack (marked by a translucent green swirl that then turns into an brass-fanfare generating instant kill if Ness's stats are high enough). If you bag a Starman Super, you net around 7500 experience and possibly the Sword of Kings. The two other enemies: less and zilch.

Your chances that a Starman Super will drop the sword? 1/128.

•

Though I was a collector (or budding hoarder; whatever you'd like to call it), I've never been a video game completist. I've always found the urge to collect every artifact and hint, every outstanding piece of the puzzle or backstory, every hat and helmet and weapon a little *wacky*. If I'm being honest, I think it's sad. For some reason, I've manufactured in my head a sort of Rubicon of video game dedication that, once crossed, removes your ability to be a functional human being. And, to me, completism's got wet boots. I always fancied myself on the relaxed, noncommittal side. The balanced side.

Let's consult the evidence, shall we?

•

A Brief and Impressionistic History of My Video Game Playing, With Many Experiences Omitted for Everyone's Sake:

EarthBound: See entire book.

Impenetrable mush of various early DOS and Atari games: I remember colors, shapes, and movement without definitive forms or objectives.

The Oregon Trail: Played it in school. Enjoyed not having to shoot animals in real life. Often played too long/was made to give up machine to other students. Estimated playtime: 200 hours.

The Incredible Machine: Built puzzles for Scott that he quickly solved; Scott built puzzles for me that I could not, in a thousand years, solve. Estimated playtime: 45 hours.

Lemmings: An early exercise in fascism. 120 hours.

Rocket Jockey: An insane and inaccurate physics lesson. 60 hours.

Duke Nukem 3D: An example of everything wrong with masculinity. A lot of fun. Scott hacked the game so the strippers would reveal their nipples. 40 hours.

Carmaggedon: Accidental preparation for living in Los Angeles. 80 hours.

Quake, Quake II: Nail guns and the Nine Inch Nails. Moody. Carcasses. Lots of hacking. Columbine. 350 hours.

Super Mario World: Wholesome. Perfect. 300 hours.

Doom, Doom II: Riveting, gruesome. Hypnotized by my avatar's face panting and becoming bloodied at the bottom of the screen as he's injured. 100 hours.

Final Fantasy III (or *VI*): Incredible. Epic. Morally and temporally complex. Worth every hour. 160 hours.

Command & Conquer: Unbelievably tense. Preparation for paying taxes in America, the Bush administration. 180 hours.

Every wrestling game ever: No comment. Too many hours.

Pokémon Red, Pokémon Blue, Pokémon Yellow: I fell in love with these games. When *Pokémon Red* and *Blue* were new, my mom, at Scott's behest, won a copy of *Pokémon Red* at a school auction with a $60 bid. Scott began playing it. I was jealous. Stole it, started playing it. Scott finished his game first but didn't seem interested; I was very, *very* interested. Played my new copy of *Red* three times, then played *Blue* twice, then *Yellow* once, having discovered every secret and caught every extant Pokémon. Began collecting and playing the card game. Found a first-edition Charizard in the first booster pack I opened. Proudly refused to trade it for a foil first-edition Alakazam and some other lame ass card. Even prouder because the man trying to trade me was over forty and held his son behind him with one stiff arm. Played various tournaments at Toys"R"Us (just looked up this spelling; holy shit, that's really how that's spelled?), won the first four badges. Around ten years old, I convinced my mom to buy me imported Japanese booster packs after successful—meaning factual—auditions in New York City. Eventually sold all my *Pokémon* cards for $1200 on eBay, getting $300 for the Charizard card alone. Undeniable evidence that I am a completist. Estimated time spent playing all *Pokémon* titles transmedia: 800 hours.

Monster Rancher Battle Card Game: Sadly seeking another *Pokémon* fix. I am not picky. 8 hours.

Wario Land: Super Mario Land 3: Fun. Remember thinking it felt "cynical," a word I was probably two years away from understanding. 20 hours.

Final Fantasy VII: Understanding that video games were quickly eating their children's lives, mom and dad made Scott and I pick either the Nintendo 64 or Playstation (not both). Don't know if they realized this was not an effective way to address the problem. We picked the Nintendo 64, so I played Playstation games at my best friends' houses. Distinctly recall playing this game for twenty-six hours in a row. Estimated playtime in total: 90 hours.

Resident Evil: Scared the shit out of me. Played this for twenty hours in a row. 60 hours.

Super Mario 64: Felt like playing a dream. 60 hours.

Mario Kart: Intensely competitive with Scott. Argued about who best performed the power slide. Absurdly pleasing glitches. 250 hours.

Goldeneye: Intensely competitive with Scott. Calculating the total hours I have played this game might drive me to suicide.

Various *Calls of* questionable *Duties*: Guns, explosions. Thoughtless killing of brown people. Cf. *Command & Conquer*. 350 hours.

The Walking Dead Game: Made me feel like shit. Potent, emotional, complicated. Impossible to navigate without feeling you've made horrendous ethical, tactical, and relational mistakes. Cf. Life. 24 hours.

And now again: *EarthBound*.

Total hours: 3,297 hours, or, if I were to play video games twelve hours per day, over 75% of one year spent playing video games (or, rather: the remarkable ones).

•

I have crossed that Rubicon.

•

So Scott and I trawled hard for that damned Sword, held by stingy and stochastic enemies.

This time I start hunting with a vague confidence that my short life's repeated lucky breaks will carry over into this game-within-a-game.

I start farming for the Sword of Kings at noon, thinking a Starman Super will drop one within the hour.

•

They.
Do.
Not.

•

At around 1:30 PM, I realize I should start counting. The SWORD OF KINGS TIPS page says that I'm likely to get the item within 45 minutes, assuming I average three slain Starman Supers per minute. I do. Roughly. (I'm still getting the hang of the spawn and respawn trick, edging out obnoxious and time-consuming Atomic Power Robots by using the Stonehenge Base's bridge's curves to trap their diamond sprites in a confused stasis.) What I do have a hang of, at this point, is going green on the Starmen and popping them into a swift, battle-less oblivion. It almost feels like a transaction: the metal symbols inch near me, I plug my sprite into them, and then I'm rewarded with some background mathematical boost. But none of these transactions give me that sweet purchase.

So I start counting aloud the number of slain Starman Super's.

One.

Two.

Three.

Oh fuck—swindled into fighting an explosive robot. *Four.*

Five.

Six. Jesus, this is tiring.

Seven …

•

Around 150, I start wondering what it feels like to be in prison.

My abductor digiti minimi muscles—the brunt-bearing wedges that support your hands as they rest on some surface while holding a SNES controller—feel like they've melted into the table.

I speak each number under my breath. The house is quiet. The animals sleep heavily. The blinds are closed. The living room is hot. I play in a rising mugginess.

Some memory-warped film projects in my internal cinema, showing a grubby Neanderthal pawing at the walls of his squalid concrete cell. He takes a bit of charcoal—down to its last vital nubbin—and makes another falling mark: | . The camera pulls back, revealing the entire wall covered in his dark scrawl, the obsessive history of his captivity and deprivation appearing to crawl over the surfaces of his cube like time-devouring ants.

One hundred and sixty-two.

•

It is 4:00 PM. I have stripped off my shirt. I have not stopped killing Starmen and Starmen Supers. I have not looked away from the screen in these hours.

How did I do it as a child? I wonder. I wonder at the use or beauty of such a game, of such a worthless pursuit. Completing what? What is gained if you find this weapon? A slight ease for the remainder of this fixed journey? A tiny, three syllable comfort?

I wonder at how some children have incredible, supra-formative capacities for repetitive activity. But no: Don't adults, too? How many of us take the same route to work every day? Eat at the same restaurants? Return, again and again, to the same body, the same charm, the same smile?

I'm not saying this part of *EarthBound* made me doubt my marriage.

I'm saying this part of *EarthBound* made me doubt the value of civilization.

•

My wife gets home and asks me how my day has been, laughing because I'm laying on our front lawn. I turn my head and smile at her, feeling the stiff grass against my back.

I tell her about the most recent problem with our health insurance. How I won't take my medicine as scheduled, after all. How I have to wait.

I then tell her that I've been killing the same video game villain for four hours in hopes of securing a rare, unnecessary tool.

I think, in that moment, of necessity. Of rarity. Of the simple, unpolished diamond in my wife's engagement ring, sheltered on its perch on her dresser. Rarely worn because of its fragility, and because of my wife's unabashed use of her hands for real stuff. Gardening, playing with dogs, etcetera.

It's when I start to vocally compare the existence of the Sword of Kings to the existence of money that I realize I must shut the fuck up and find the thing already.

•

Two hundred and fifty-eight battles later, the Starman Super drops it.

I shout, "YES!"

My wife cheers from the other room. Half-jokingly, she says, "I'm proud of you, babe."

I laugh, and find the Sword in the menu screen. I equip it.

I stare at the screen for a moment, a rat in thrall to the button.

Ready to press through to the end.

•

But there are also moments of irretrievable beauty in video games. Ephemeral glitches that point to the sublime. Randomized variables that are made more poetic in their expression by their adjacency to the rote and to the banal.

In Winters, before the Sword of Kings excursion, I neared the edge of the water. And there, hovering over the blue, was a Magic Butterfly.

Throughout the game, you encounter these flitting salves. If you can catch one, it floats up both sides of your body, bestowing a gift of relaxation (i.e. health and psychic powers). Its gift given, it blinks out of existence after a flash of lavender.

And there it was, hovering over the water just one step east of Tessie's isthmus, unmoving save for its flapping wings.

•

After shutting down the Stonehenge Base, rescuing its human test subjects, and curing the shyness of a tribe of protozoan cave dwellers, Ness, Paula, Jeff, and Poo jump into a hole. The resulting dungeon is unremarkable and its boss inconsequential. What it guards, though, is anything but.

Lumine Hall is a cavernous corridor, its walls a living, scrolling earthbound Lite-Brite. After a moment, a smooth stretch of wall starts speaking. Speaking via scrolling text, that is, like a city bus's destination sign. That regular method now relit in this sacred context.

I'm Ness … It's been a long road getting here … Soon, I'll be … Soon, I'll be … Soon, I'll be … What will happen to us? W … what's happening? My thoughts are being written out on the wall … or are they?

The text disappears, and Ness catches a glimpse of his father holding him as a baby.

Though mostly silent, *EarthBound* doesn't paint its heroes as overconfident. They get ill, homesick, paralyzed, tired, lost, kidnapped. The game's difficulty appears in the cracks formed by the fracture of its central team. Its characters are curious, hopeful, dedicated, but they are not unfeeling. They are not blood-drenched barbarians, or ancient warriors. They are kids. Kids woken in the night by a meteor, and by unfamiliar hands, and by calls for help. They all shoulder a massive, increasingly costly burden. They are invited to destroy themselves and depart from their bodies for the sake of a promise.

Lumine Hall, to me, reminds me of all the hidden potential in a healthy child. Even if a child's parents are poor or geographically stranded, a child can live within an imaginative realm of transformation and experience, all shifting with and within his or her whims, morphing in and out of fantasy at the speed of thought. I marvel at the distance that a kid's mind can cover, navigating such disparate and promising realms.

EarthBound, like all good art, can work as a sieve. The child's rough, unlimited desires can reach a finer grain with its help. *EarthBound*, in its thematic width and variety, and in its emotional openness and honesty, forms a uniquely powerful shape that you or I can fill with our attention and further fantasy. Like Lumine Hall, the game is a sanctuary in which you can see yourself connected to and reflected by its simple structure.

It's as simple as: a cave meets a Lite-Brite.

It's as simple as: soon, I'll be …
Soon, I'll be …
Soon, I'll be …

•

At the end of Lumine Hall, you jump into another hole, this time falling into the Earth and backwards through time. After a beat, the screen fades up, and your entire party is three pixels tall.

The Lost Underworld projects the reality that it's *EarthBound*'s largest level, but it's also the most straightforward. After fending off dinosaurs, interfacing with talking rocks, and battling a shapeshifting dog, you reach your eighth and final Sanctuary: a lava-spewing mini volcano, its magma flowing down a seemingly endless cliff.

After struggling so long, the vital music coalesces. Finally piecing together *EarthBound*'s eight-part melody, Ness falls unconscious.

•

The screen fades up to a black-and-white image of a younger Ness, deliberately walking up a winding, lonely path. A nursery rhyme version of *EarthBound*'s central melody plays. Ness reaches the door of his house, moored to the end of this dreamlike bridge, and he dissolves. After a moment, our point-of-view is that of a spirit roaming through Ness's childhood home. We float across the living room, down the upstairs hallway, through the door. In the middle of Ness's room is a rocking bassinet. We overhear a conversation between Ness's mother and father as they admire their child together and notice the peculiar movement of a baby bottle that he's pointing to.

It's an odd moment, both uncanny and wholesome (which might be the most succinct way to describe *EarthBound*'s entire tone). It also serves as a hint at *EarthBound*'s earliest influences—in an early interview about the game, Shigesato Itoi said:

"Everyone would get together to watch shows like *Lucy, Gunsmoke, Flipper, The Beverly Hillbillies* and *Twilight Zone*. That was our picture of America—*Father Knows Best* and *Leave It To Beaver*. I love to think of America as a place like that."

EarthBound's gentle idealism, though honest in its depiction of the spread of evil, could only have been born out of a rosy reading of a distant culture. The manicured lawns, well-paid jobs, and respectful proms of America were girded with the post-war spoils of World War II's productive boom. America, in the wake of such a massive, global atrocity, looked like a peaceful place. It's easy to see how Itoi could admire it, especially the carefully constructed fantasy of America presented on television—a fantasy built by writers ultimately paid to stoke the viewer's desire to consume, a desire that Itoi grew up to stoke professionally and profit greatly by doing so. Those programs and their commercials depicted America as a place of wholesome antics and heroic deeds. America, then, was the hardened warrior back at home with his family, warmed but distant, far from the bomb, and just happy to put his feet up and watch some television.

•

After this monochromatic scene, Ness wakes up in Magicant, a shapeshifting Euclidean fantasia sustained by Ness's memory.

You can speak to stranded characters from your journey: rabbit statues from Dalaam, Paula's preschool friends, zombies, punks, and even Pokey. Some still feel the pain from your beating. Some are happy to live inside this dreamland. Some want your forgiveness, your friendship.

You speak to a snowman, perpetually frosty in the chamber of Ness's memory.

He says: "Thank you for remembering me."

•

Today, humans consume, produce, and reproduce so rapidly that we're close to irreparably destabilizing Earth's climate and ability to sustain life (if we haven't already). Even the most conservative scientific evidence is overwhelmingly doomy. According to Stephen Emmott, author of the recent book *Ten Billion*, "We need to consume less. A lot less. Less food, less energy, less stuff. Fewer cars, electric cars, cotton T-shirts, laptops, mobile phone upgrades. Far fewer." In *Ten Billion*, Emmott—head of Microsoft's Computational Science research into complex systems—reviews the growing body of ecological evidence then concludes with this: "We urgently need to do—and I mean actually do—something radical to avert a global catastrophe. But I don't think we will ... I think we're fucked."

What does that radical action look like? Reproducing less and curtailing our consumption are two obvious parts of the solution, so wouldn't it also be wise to produce and consume less art and entertainment? Attention has proven to be an exhaustible and highly commodified resource. Although it isn't a causal factor, many societies have developed a taste for complex art and spectacle on the eve of radical collapse. So might we also need to produce art that is less reliant on increasingly costly infrastructure?

In the last few years, it's become commonplace to slow down popular songs and present them as new entities. For example, the *Jurassic Park* theme sounds magnificently unfamiliar when slowed a thousand percent. Beethoven's *9th Symphony* can be listened to in the form of a sonic, eternal molasses, slowed to last twenty-four hours. *Jolene*, Dolly Parton's classic ballad, takes on a sultry, sexually ambiguous tone when slowed to 33rpm. Each sounds novel, re-discoverable.

The desire to express ourselves is as deep a part of most of us as the desire to reproduce, if you can even consider them separate; like bowerbirds that build elaborate blue nests to dazzle potential mates, our desire for self-expression may finally be subsumed into the simple drive to go forth and multiply.

Then could these middle works—art pulled from the past, transformed, then re-presented—be considered a necessary step between making complex recorded art built to spread and simple ephemeral art that leaves no trace?

In a 2008, director Darren Aronofsky was asked if his films were comments on how much of ourselves we should devote to our work. He responded:

"It's not becoming an either/or. It's becoming about living life as an art. Because I think that line is artificial, is kind of what I'm learning. Making product is not really the end-result. In fact it might be a fake result. It might be a mistake. It's a whole kinda capitalistic critique, but the amount of destruction that a film does to the environment is remarkable. Sure it can do great good, but I think about the amount of chemicals that come out of the amount of footage I shoot. So actually making physical products is questionable, I think. I think it's dangerous, ultimately. I think we should all be dancers and performance artists. I think that's probably a better form of expression."

So we ban the blockbusters and wipe away the CGI spectacles. We think less in light show and more in black box (or black cave). How might this response to our ecological problems apply to games?

Instead of making another three hundred million dollar game where you murder brown people for twelve hours, maybe we should go back to already-extant games like *EarthBound*.

Or chess.

Or, if we're honest: hide and go seek.

•

Hide and go seek being played—unintentionally and fatally—in the Japanese film *House*.

Recently, after laying on a friend's couch and regaling him with anecdotes about *EarthBound*'s plot and general weirdness, I asked him my stock question, praying for a new answer: "What sounds similar to *EarthBound*, to you? Could be anything—a movie, game, book. Anything." At this point, because it had happened four times already, I expected him to point out *EarthBound*'s similarities to another story about a prophesied young boy who, with the help of his friends and their magic powers, saves the world from evil: Harry Potter. But after a second, my friend said, "Have you seen *House*?"

House is a Japanese film theatrically released in 1977, and I had not. That night, I sat down and watched it.

•

I'll start by saying that *House* features the most nonchalantly rendered instance of cat telekinesis I have ever seen.

The moment comes early on in the film, although in *House*, time isn't really an organizing principle (the fuzzy white cat's eyes gleam green, then weird shit happens). This is maybe the only reliable, structured event in the whole film, and it's followed by a teen girl's body dissolving in a flash flood of what resembles red Koolaid, another teen girl who gets concurrently sexed and dismembered by a haunted piano, and another teen girl getting beaten to death with futon mattresses and then turned into a doll.

Watching *House* feels like living in a manic child's brain, which makes sense because the film's director took a bunch of ideas from his ten-year old daughter and told *House's* screenwriter to use them. The edits—transitions in the film's thought—are erratic, nonsensical. The lighting—the film's mood—is sugary and irreal. And the direction—the film's logic, rationality, and self-narrative—is playful, sappy, hysterical, pained, and crazily inventive.

House's director, Nobuhiko Obayashi, worked mainly as a commercial director. After the success of *Jaws*, Japanese studios hastily wanted to recreate the film's success, thinking that it was spawned solely by an auteur's youthful (and commercial) enthusiasm. Nobuhiko convinced Toho, a large Japanese film studio, to greenlight *House*, but wouldn't yet put up the required budget. Leveraging the greenlight's publicity, Obayashi launched a multimedia assault, presenting *House* to the Japanese public as a radio play, novel, manga, and official soundtrack to the yet-to-be-filmed film. Finally, Toho succumbed and fronted the money.

Watching *House* for the first time, I was struck by the similarities between its main melody and *Earth-Bound's*. And now, comparing the scores side by side, it's clear they're kin. Another likeness, or nod: At that time, it was considered taboo in Japan to title a Japanese film with an English word. Another oddly English title: *Mother*.

House was a huge hit when it was first released; might Shigesato Itoi have been influenced by *House*'s unlikely success? Itoi was twenty-eight when *House* came out in 1977, and only a few years away from his peak popularity as a copywriter. Maybe he saw it, and maybe he felt charged by it. Maybe *House*'s sense of radical permission took hold of Itoi when he first considered how *Mother* might feel.

While I enjoyed *House*'s hyper-slapstick version of a ghost story, it doesn't feel as explorative or cohesive as *EarthBound*. As its end credits rolled, I sat on my couch feeling lonely. I was anthropomorphizing *EarthBound*, and I felt that he/she was still stranded in singularity. It's a weird game, and my admiration for it felt reproachable, as if I was the sole friend of the kid who nobody in school wants to hang out with because of his spazzy gait.

•

After venturing to the heart of Magicant, you are again met with the glimmering Mani Mani statue (which I now realize is—save for its thin, beetle-esque horns—identical to the Oscar statuette). The golden idol, now dubbed Ness's Nightmare, rests on a small rock platform in the kraken-cut, purple waters of the Sea of Eden. It incarnates the evil in Ness's heart, and it waits for you to destroy it

In the 25th chapter of Exodus, God's mountaintop request for bling, obedience, and worship from Moses and the children of Israel begins with:

> Speak unto the children of Israel, that they bring me an offering: of every man that giveth it willingly with his heart ye shall take my offering.
>
> And this is the offering which ye shall take of them; gold, and silver, and brass,
>
> And blue, and purple, and scarlet, and fine linen, and goats' hair,
>
> And rams' skins dyed red, and badgers' skins, and shittim wood,
>
> Oil for the light, spices for anointing oil, and for sweet incense,
>
> Onyx stones, and stones to be set in the ephod, and in the breastplate.
>
> And let them make me a sanctuary; that I may dwell among them.

And blue, and purple, and scarlet.

Happy Happy Village, the Sea of Eden, and the oncoming fight with Giygas, fleshed by a chaotic red.

•

According to the Star Master, *EarthBound*'s ancient guru, "The Sea of Eden is filled with ultimate intelligence. You can't go there unless you're truly ready. It's a place where you can touch the truth of the universe. Going there may bring sorrow."

For Ness, the journey within ends in a universal truth: at the center of the sea of intelligence stands a glimmering evil.

This knowledge, like the storied Fall from innocence in the Sea of Eden's earthly counterpart, or the sudden self-consciousness at the terminus of youth, is often linked with sorrow. But must they be?

Can they be split?

•

Ness, newly empowered by defeating his inner evil, wakes. You guide him and his party back to Saturn Valley, but are told that in order to travel through time to confront Gigyas, you must first return home to retrieve a piece of the meteor that first woke you.

Onett is now cast in perpetual night and haunted by deadly entities. Your family cowers in their house, terrified, trapped.

After retrieving a piece of the meteor, you return to Saturn Valley. Using a device called the Phase Distorter, you travel deep within the Earth, but find that Giygas is absent. According to prophecy, Giygas conquers Earth ten years in the future, but you discover that he is currently attacking from this place but from innumerable years in the past.

To reach this temporal triple-threat, though, you must be disembodied, your consciousness ported to individualized robots capable of time-travel. The fear about the consequences of this procedure—that you won't be able to return to your body—is expressed to you by your doctor and Jeff's father.

It is *EarthBound*'s final metaphysical gambit.

Supine and eyes closed, your body vibrates under the audible strain of drills and sparking equipment.

•

Three months before Aviva and I were to be married, I was hospitalized for fourteen days.

After months of careless eating and mounting stress, I began to feel pain in my stomach. Initially I ignored it, thinking it would go away on its own, but it didn't; it became more intense, diffuse, and unpredictable. Eating was painful, then so was peeing. For five nights in a row, I woke in terrible pain with a fever of 104°. I was limping to compensate for a steady pain between my right leg and my abdomen. I was waiting to see a gastroenterologist in Pasadena who could only see me a month from then, but fearing that I wouldn't make it that long, my fiancé called the most experienced gastroenterologist at Cedars-Sinai and pleaded for them to see me that day. When I visited the office, the physician's assistant told me to turn around and go straight to the ER. By morning, my ER doctor told me there was a hole in my small intestine that had led to the formation of a large abscess on my psoas muscle, an abscess that would've burst in about a day.

This began a two-month long process of hospitalizations, minor and major surgeries, complex medication regimens, constant eating to stabilize my weight, and an all-pervasive *holy shit—I'm severely ill* anxiety.

The first line of defense against what my doctors soon diagnosed as a severe, perforative case of Crohn's disease was to drain the abscess. This involved two adults drilling a hole in my abdomen and forcibly threading a thin wire into me while I was fully awake. My doctors then sent me home with an abdominal catheter (draining into a bag strapped to my leg; *hello, ladies ...*) and a stiff course of antibiotics, opioid pain-killers, and mood-wrecking steroids. For five days, I ate, ate, ate, ate, and ate while sitting on the couch and lying in bed, constantly cared for by my fiancé and my mom. After a few days, though, we noticed that my catheter wasn't draining anymore.

With Aviva and Mom holding me up by my arms, I limped into the surgeon's office. He told us what I expected him to tell us: I needed major abdominal surgery and I needed it immediately. We left his office and parked on a side-street so my mom could call my dad. She started crying, so she walked a few houses down the street, leaving me and Aviva in the car. The sun was gorgeous; the day purely lit. I was in the passenger seat and I turned around to face my bride-to-be. "I know this is going to be hard, but I want us to talk about me dying."

We cried while I asked her to say aloud that she would find happiness without me.

THE CAVE OF THE PAST

I ENTER THE cave as the temperature outside my house reaches 100°.

The cave's walkways are crystalline, perfectly flat, sea-gray. The edges of its navigable paths are minutely fractal, the only hint of the natural world inside Giygas's cold preface. Its enemies—dark, point-cut diamonds—frantically haunt its space, never touching the ground. Fights are unforgiving—you're flashed to death, paralyzed, racked with unavoidable explosive damage. You're left to heal, then heal, then heal again. Your souls—evacuated from your bodies by a vibratory operation only signaled by the sound of drills and sparks of light—are as fragile as your new metallic frames. Your steps clunk against the cave's smooth alien floor. Time is not this world's organizing principle: It is power, evil, trauma.

You open the world's sole gift box and receive the game's last weapon, the Legendary Bat.

You walk north.

•

Giygas's final chamber is called the Devil Machine.

It is made of a twisting path of throbbing entrails set inside the deep, cavernous breaths of your unseen enemy. Giygas, offscreen, in repose. The dragon at slumber.

You reach the apex of this machine and face it, its appearance more computational than living, as if the heavily tubed entity was built for catastrophic thinking. Its center console is a soft, blank, dented eye. An organ yet to reveal its purpose.

You approach it.

The entire machine wobbles, shimmying as it dimly reveals its face to you: and its face is yours.

Ness.

Placid, unblinking. The face of the bodied boy, though, only a husk in a distant valley.

You face yourself for a moment—facing the evidence of your life; as much truth as a mirror can accommodate—before Pokey appears. Spider-like in a mechanized, semi-organic machine of his own, his face the pale blue of the newly dead and wrenched into a sneer.

The fight begins.

Your threshold for pain decided by the work you have done before.

You hurt Pokey enough to risk turning off the Devil's Machine, releasing Giygas' power from its bounds. Now you face pure evil, unable to think rationally, unable to sense itself.

You face this evil in its dementia, and follow it into further formless, rabid madnesses. You beat it out of its only structures. The chaotic decrepitude narrated by Pokey's taunts: "And here you stand, waiting to be burned up with all the rest of the garbage of this universe ..."

Giygas, now split and drifting in a mindless, measureless fluid, attacks you only with an unknowable force. Your minds are unable to grasp the true form of its attacks. You are hurt. Your heroes are killed.

This evil is seemingly endlessly alive, though: Your attacks are useless.

Giygas mumbles, repeats your name, cries that it is being wronged, moans in pleasure, in pain.

What is left?

Your tools are useless. Your body is useless.

•

My mom driving me to and from the hospital. My wife siting me up in bed. My mom slowly lowering me to sit on the toilet. My wife bathing me, cleaning my wounds. Feeding me. Singing me to sleep.

•

So you pray.

•

It is a simple act.
You close your eyes. You may speak, or you may not.
And in this case, with nothing else left, you ask for help.

•

And this plea transcends time, somehow whole and spirited enough to leave this mutating void.
It reaches those waiting in Saturn Valley. They hear it, feel it. They cast you in their thoughts.
And, miraculously, Giygas begins to crumble.

•

You pray.

A nameless concern reaches the Runaway Five, and they join in prayer for your safety.

Giygas is hurt once more.

You pray.

Paula's parents stop and fervently pray for their daughter's wellbeing.

Its evil is hurt.

You pray.

Jeff's friends gather in their cold common area and pray through their shared anxiety.

And hurt again.

You pray.

A young woman in Dalaam wakes from a dream of Poo's death and then prays for his life.

Again.

You pray.

Franky, the former boss of Onett's gang, recalls Ness's face and begins to pray for this old enemy.

You pray.

Ness's mother, and sister, and pet dog all gather in the night, in fear for their son's, brother's, and companion's life. In response, they do all they can. They pray.

Giygas is harmed again, but deeply harmed, sent now into a staticky loop of aggressive noise and movement.

Broken into thousands of shifting, tensile harms.
You pray again.
But your call is absorbed by the darkness.

•

You must.

•

You pray again.

•

And then you, reading right now, are named.
You are brought into this fight by your common sign.
You pray for these kids, having never met them.
And it hits Giygas.
Hard.

•

You keep praying.
Your strength doubles.
You keep praying.
Your might doubles again. As strong as you ever will be.
Are you praying for Ness?
Paula?

Jeff?

Poo?

Are you praying for strength against the world's evils?

•

Please:

Close your eyes and ask for help.

I know this may feel silly, but it doesn't have to. As someone alive only because of a confluence of circumstances so singular and complex that it is impossible to understand, do you think it silly to acknowledge that union? With your mind? Your voice?

And if you don't find it silly, then why not speak to that fate in a humble way?

•

You can ask for help from the god you worship. You can ask if you're unable to name one at all. You can ask without expecting an answer.

You can ask solely to know that you are wounded and that you are here.

•

Ask for your safety, for your victories, for forgiveness, empathy, and understanding.

Ask for help, for order, for life.

Ask for the world to thrive without you.

Ask to be given access to old graces, and ask to be able to make new ones.

Please:

I will do it with you:

Let's close our eyes and ask.

HOME

GIYGAS' FINAL FORM is static.

The stochastic, frenzied noise of the universe distilled into something seeable and hearable. Static—*exerting force by reason of weight alone without motion*—as the terminal, foundational form of all.

This is what you've reduced this intelligence to. This will. You've flattened *EarthBound*'s evil into the non-qualitative process out of which life arose.

Finally, it collapses into itself, and into black.

Perhaps the precursor to a big bang.

•

After the battle, Ness, Paula, Jeff and Poo are restored to their bodies in Saturn Valley.

•

After regaining the ability to walk on my own, I went back to work. I had been gone for a month. The soundstage air was still when I entered, the cast and crew hushed. I thanked everyone for their messages of concern, their gifts, and their patience. And then, to really let everyone know that I was okay, I made a fart joke. Laughing with everyone—and feeling the tiny pains in my healing abdomen—felt incredible.

When I got home from that first day back, before opening my front door, I turned around and watched the massive sycamore tree across the street. The wind moved through it; it moved in turn. Alive. Upright.

Miraculous.

•

Jeff and Poo each depart with a sentimental goodbye. You're left with Paula, who asks you to escort her home.

After dropping her off, you're left to explore the entire world of *EarthBound*. You can ride your bike through the swamps of the Deep Darkness and listen to the weird sounds this travel makes. You can buy the seaside house in Onett and discover its wrecked interior, the home missing its far-facing wall, open to the odorless salted air, its dresser containing an odd short story readable only by you. You can return *Overcoming*

Shyness to Onett's librarian and get a kiss in return. You can spend hours talking to every NPC in the game, many who say new stuff, their lives changed by your legendary triumph. The world has changed and progressed in some fundamental way. It is a world without evil and without common enemy. A world holding in the pristine harmony that comes before it splits and coalesces to seek new evils.

•

Alive and able-bodied again, I explore the world.

The peace feels lonely.

After awhile, I guide Ness home. We walk over to his mother, and I press the button that leads him to perform *EarthBound*'s last feat: Sitting down together and looking at photos of your journey.

It's a fitting end to the central game in the Mother franchise, and one that is much more beautiful to me now—aware of my friends and family's sacrifices for me—than as a child.

•

EarthBound's grandest act is self-transcendence.

As Ness, you must give up the comforting regularity of your childhood to save humanity. But to do so, you need the help of three friends. Paula leaves the bubble of her local popularity as a gifted child in order to accompany Ness, a fellow psychic who saves her from captivity. Paula and Ness are then trapped and must rely on a physically transcendent plea for help to reach Jeff, who has pursued scientific excellence in lieu of a normal childhood's free play since he was a little boy. And then comes Poo, who must transcend the most basic human desire—self-preservation—to fully realize his powers and join you. Together you face a Giygas, the ultimate schizophrenic evil, but not before having your very *beings* separated from your bodies and inserted into makeshift shells. In the final confrontation, it does not matter how powerful you are; again you are left with no other option but to ask for help from your family, your friends, strangers, and, finally, *you*, the unseen player. It takes a multitude in prayer to defeat Giygas. The challenge finally over, you return to your bodies and can explore the world in solemnity. The game's last act—the last event that you can enact with a press of a button—is sitting down with your mother and showing her photographs of your journey. Transcendence by way of storytelling.

By sharing memories.

•

But there's so much more.

There's *Mother 3*, the sequel that many feel is even more impactful and masterful than *EarthBound*.

There's the fan-made *Mother 4*, which recently debuted a promising trailer online and is slated to come out in late 2014.

There's the *Mother 2* novelization, written by Saori Kumi and painstakingly translated into English by Lindsay Nelson.

And there are the thousands of pages of literature about *EarthBound*—theories, quirks, impressions, psychological and mythical analyses, guides, essays, and reviews—and thousands and thousands of pieces of art depicting its universe—music, paintings, drawings, movies, sculpture, and homemade fashions—as well as the homebrew hacks that let you play lovingly altered versions of the story.

Now, in the age of cultural abundance, you never have to finish a game.

The window of play is only closed by that final stiff breeze.

•

Some video games will outlive us.

I hope *EarthBound* lives to be played after I'm gone.

•

EarthBound has been resuscitated.

During the first month of its rerelease, *EarthBound* is the third bestselling game in the Wii U eShop, trailing only the new *Luigi* and *Pikmin* games.

Fresh and praiseful reviews are popping up at the largest and most eyeballed video game websites, essays about the game being published, podcasts and gameplay sessions are being recorded, and gaming legends like developer Tim Schafer are ecstatically tweeting through their first playthrough.

•

Upon the rerelease, Shigesato Itoi wrote this message to the game's fans. In it, he talks about how he has changed since making the game, and how he thinks about what kind of person he wants to be when he dies: "someone with a lively wake."

> The person who passed away has to be in all sorts of different people's memories.
> What they've done, how stupid they were, what kind of things they did for fun,
> and how kind that person was sometimes.
> All the people who are still alive are laughing,
> wanting to be the first one to bring up those things to everyone around them.

The life I want to live is something that can be concluded with that kind of a party-like wake.

Fame and fortune, setting records and accomplishments are all meaningless.

That person is inside those stories that are told, where people talk about their episodes, casually and sincerely.

Well, it's not dead, and it's not even human, but to me *Earthbound* is a game that's kind of like that guy.

•

Because of this book, Scott and I are talking again. We text nearly every day about whatever comes to mind—everyday stuff: jokes, pictures of beautiful stuff, or recent enthusiasms for a new game or movie or book—and we plan to see each other in person soon after my wife and I move to Santa Fe.

Because of this book, I met Scott again—a person full of generosity, discipline, tenderness, passion, respect.

Now, unmoored from the stasis of my memories, Scott *feels* like family.

•

EarthBound isn't just an incredible memory from my childhood, and it's not only a strong wellspring for my nostalgia; *EarthBound* is a game made whole by its jokes and its peacefulness, by its references and poignancies, and by its lessons, challenges, and thrills. It is made completely alive by its variety and its familiarity.

EarthBound feels like family, too.

NOTES

199X

1. The version of *Ornament and Crime* that I first read: http://bit.ly/1bE0mTm (PDF)
2. A great overview of Shigesato Itoi's copywriting: http://bit.ly/1bxz548 (Yomuka)

EAGLELAND

1. Here's that racist *Tom Sawyer* adaptation: http://bit.ly/1bvX405 (Wikipedia)
2. Jung's essay on synchronicities can be found in this gorgeously produced translation of the *I Ching*: http://amzn.to/18UyUCh (Amazon)
3. More on Starmen.net's staggering *Mother 3* petition: http://bit.ly/1f7k7m8 (Starmen)
4. Itoi on *The Military Policeman and the Dismembered Beauty*: http://bit.ly/18D16aa (EarthBound Central)
5. Nick Paumgarten's excellent profile of Shigeru Miyamoto at *The New Yorker*: http://nyr.kr/1jO3SOB (*New Yorker*)

Onett

1. Although many are available online, the Zen koans are gleaned from from Katsuki Sekida's great translations of *The Gateless Gate* and *The Blue Cliff Records*: amzn.to/1bvXp2R (Amazon)

2. Re: "aggressive neural activity" and "one study butts up against": http://bit.ly/1gpLPOQ (Media Psychology PDF)

3. Re: "improved cognitive abilities ... in elderly folks": http://on.wsj.com/IPCNf7 (*Wall Street Journal*)

4. On the cultural differences between the violence schizophrenic patients hear: http://nyti.ms/1f7kIo1 (*New York Times*)

5. If this book leads you to read one other book, let it be *Straw Dogs* by John Gray: http://amzn.to/19Ccv75 (Amazon)

6. That translation of the Heraclitus line is by Brooks Haxton in this edition: http://amzn.to/1bE1Xsg (Amazon)

Twoson

1. Legends of Localization's EarthBound site – http://bit.ly/J6t-doB – is an incredibly thorough compendium and one of the most fascinating sites that I've researched for this book. If you enjoy the challenges or mysteries of literary or cross-cultural translation, or if you give a shit about the lingual building blocks of *EarthBound*, Legends of Localization will titillate.

2. And I'm not the first person to dwell on *EarthBound*'s connection to JonBenét Ramsey. *Doll Doll Doll*, an album by the Canadian electronic musician Venetian Snares—an album that, according to Wikipedia, is "extremely dark, themed largely around the murder of children"—samples the answering machine message for the information line regarding JonBenét's

investigation in the song "Dollmaker" and errant tones from *EarthBound*'s score in the song "Remi."

3. *DNA: The Ultimate Hard Drive* by John Bohannon: http://bit.ly/1cBdLvv (*Science Mag*)

4. Re: the amount of DNA a human body contains: http://to.pbs.org/19hAyvL (PBS)

5. On Fusako Sano: http://bit.ly/1iWYM4o (*Japan Times*), http://bbc.in/1hMNwX3 (BBC), http://bit.ly/1jO5wjc (Amarillo)

6. *Bluets* by Maggie Nelson: http://bit.ly/1aViX8Y (Wave Books)

7. Lindblom on dodging KKK allusions: http://wrd.cm/1f7ltxd (*Wired*)

8. The source of Rumsfeld's snakelike philosophy lesson: http://1.usa.gov/IFyaER (defense.gov)

THREED

1. A great video from Kotaku on *EarthBound*'s musical influences & nods: http://bit.ly/1hMNNcm (Kotaku)

2. Itoi & Iwata's conversation about game-making: http://bit.ly/1d8bE0s (1101.com)

3. Itoi on Jeff's sexuality: http://bit.ly/JeH78E (EarthBound Central)

4. Overviews of the changing Japanese family and the differences between Japanese & American men's parenting: http://bit.ly/18UA6pc (Google), http://bit.ly/18BXAtw (*The Guardian*), http://bit.ly/1kzLhmY (ncfr.org)

5. Itoi on parenting and *Mother 4*: http://bit.ly/1f7m1Dn (EarthBound Central)

6. On *EarthBound*'s marketing campaign: http://bit.
   ly/1jO6HPC (EarthBound Central), http://bit.ly/1f7m6a2
   (EarthBound Central)

FOURSIDE

1. Comparing video game maps: http://bit.ly/1bvYqIa (Wikipedia), http://bit.ly/1hMO9zL (Giant Bomb), http://bit.
   ly/1bE6aMC (Imgur)
2. The Oakwood Child Actor Project: http://bit.ly/1bWLGR2
   (Oakwood.com)
3. The *Japan Times* profile of Itoi: http://bit.ly/J6uQCD (*Japan
   Times*)
4. The Hobonichi quote belongs to Shigesato Itoi, August 15th
   being the day Japan surrendered in 1945.
5. Michel McBride-Charpentier's overview of the critical literature on *EarthBound*: http://bit.ly/1gpqNjo (Critical Distance)
6. The "Heroin, carbohydrates, and a monthly salary" aphorism
   is from Nassim Nicholas Taleb's vital *The Bed of Procrustes*:
   http://amzn.to/1jOc29J (Amazon)

DEEP DARKNESS

1. The infernal guide: http://bit.ly/IPFygl (Starmen)
2. *Ten Billion* by Stephen Emott: http://amzn.to/1iX3IGF (Amazon)
3. Itoi on *EarthBound* and his admiration for 50's American TV:
   http://bit.ly/1f7jQzN (Earthbound Central)

4. For a rigorously empirical study of collapsing societies, see *The Collapse of Complex Societies* by Joseph Tainter: http://amzn.to/19hzic4 (Amazon)

5. Manuel DeLanda speaks beautifully of bowerbirds during this talk about the philosophy of Gilles Deleuze: bit.ly/1d8aK3W (YouTube)

6. Darren Aronofsky feeling bad about ecology: bit.ly/1iWWu5n (KCRW)

7. All info about *House* came from *Constructing a "House,"* the behind-the-scenes documentary on the Criterion Collection edition: http://bit.ly/1coGMHs (Criterion)

8. Do I really need to cite the King James Bible?

HOME

1. I owe a bow to Darius Kazemi and Starmen.net for their attention to *EarthBound*'s dénouement: bit.ly/J6mTNX (Tiny Subversions), bit.ly/1bWGSLw (Starmen)

2. In the house you can buy in Onett, the short story in the dresser is in a magazine called *My Secret Life*; the television show that I worked on for five years—and that paid enough for me to buy my house—was called *The Secret Life of the American Teenager*. Another wormhole.

3. Itoi's message to *EarthBound* fans upon the game's North American rerelease: bit.ly/1aVg4oK (Nintendo)

ACKNOWLEDGEMENTS

DEEP BROTHERLY GRATITUDE to Gabe Durham, who said "I'll start Boss Fight Books if you write the first book," dealt with my Kickstarter mania, let me design the series, then greatly improved this book through his editorial guidance and our long conversations between smoothies. And thank you to Marcus Lindblom, Daniel Lisi, Lisa Ladehoff, Kaitlyn Martin, Constantine Sandis, Lindsay Nelson, Clyde Mandelin, the Starmen.net community, Shigesato Itoi, and the rest. And of course, an indelible and endless thanks to my family. You have all saved me.

SPECIAL THANKS

FOR MAKING THIS series possible, Boss Fight Books would like to thank Andrew Thivyanathan, Carolyn Kazemi, Cathy Durham, Ken Durham, Maxwell Neely-Cohen, Jack Brounstein, Andres Chirino, Adam J. Tarantino, Ronald Irwin, Rachel Mei, Raoul Fesquet, Gaelan D'costa, Nicolas-Loic Fortin, Tore Simonsen, Anthony McDonald, Ricky Steelman, Daniel Joseph Lisi, Ann Loyd, Warren G. Hanes, Ethan Storeng, Tristan Powell, and Joe Murray.

COMING SOON
FROM
BOSS FIGHT
BOOKS

CPSIA information can be obtained at www.ICGtesting.com
Printed in the USA
LVOW06s0921270514

387333LV00004B/5/P